CAMPAIGN 340

THE GLORIOUS FIRST OF JUNE 1794

MARK LARDAS

ILLUSTRATED BY EDOUARD GROULT

Series Editor Marcus Cowper

OSPREY
Bloomsbury Publishing Plc
PO Box 883, Oxford, OX1 9PL, UK
1385 Broadway, 5th Floor, New York, NY 10018, USA
E-mail: info@ospreypublishing.com
www.ospreypublishing.com

OSPREY is a trademark of Osprey Publishing Ltd

First published in Great Britain in 2019

A catalogue record for this book is available from the British Library.

ISBN: PB 9781472834843; eBook 9781472834850; ePDF 9781472834836; XML 9781472834867

19 20 21 22 23 10 9 8 7 6 5 4 3 2 1

Maps by Bounford.com
3D BEVs by The Black Spot
Index by Fionbar Lyons
Typeset by PDQ Digital Media Solutions, Bungay, UK
Printed and bound in India by Replika Press Private Ltd.

Osprey Publishing supports the Woodland Trust, the UK's leading woodland conservation charity.

To find out more about our authors and books, visit **www.ospreypublishing.com**. Here you will find extracts, author interviews, details of forthcoming events and the option to sign up for our newsletter.

DEDICATION

I dedicated my first book to my father and his father, my paternal grandfather. These two did more to instil a love of the sailing era than anyone else. That was in 2003. While my grandfather had died a quarter of a century earlier, my father, Nicholas Lardas, was alive. Over the last 15 years he was my biggest booster and fan, helping me with several books. He was looking forward to this one with more than usual enthusiasm. It was another sailing-era book. He never saw more than a few rough outlines of this one. Shortly after I started work on it, Dad died, a week before his 95th birthday.
This one is for my father. Dad, I will miss you.

ACKNOWLEDGEMENTS

I would like to thank Rama Neko for allowing me access to his library of images.

AUTHOR'S NOTE

The following abbreviations indicate the sources of the illustrations used in this volume:
AC – Author's Collection
LOC – Library of Congress, Washington, D.C.
Rama – Rama Neko
USNHHC – United States Navy Heritage and History Command

KEY TO BIRD'S-EYE VIEWS

French/British frigate

French/British ship-of-the-line

French/British ship-of-the-line, partially dismasted

French/British ship-of-the-line, completely dismasted

French ship-of-the-line, towed to safety by frigate

PREVIOUS PAGE
The battle fought on 1 June was the first major fleet action of the French Revolutionary Wars. It was also one of the biggest, with over 50 ships-of-the-line taking part. (AC)

CONTENTS

Strategic Overview

Map legend:

- - - - - - Expected track of the grain convoy

GREAT BRITAIN

Cape Clear
Ireland (British)
Cork ●

London ●
Plymouth ●
Portsmouth ●
The Lizard
English Channel

FRANCE

Paris ●

Brest ●
Ushant
Belle Île
Rochefort ●
Bay of Biscay
Cape Ortegal
Cape Finisterre

SPAIN

PORTUGAL

Toulon ●

N

0 — 100 miles
0 — 100km

Off map

1. 10 April: Rochefort Squadron sails.
2. 11 April: Grain Convoy departs the Chesapeake.
3. 12 April: Channel Fleet sails.
4. 9 May: Rochefort Squadron encounters and captures HMS *Castor* and the Newfoundland Convoy.
5. 7 May: *Atalante* captured by HMS *Swiftsure*.
6. 17 May: Brest Fleet sails.
7. 17 May: Brest Fleet and Channel Fleet pass each other in the fog.
8. 19 May: Brest Fleet encounters and captures the Lisbon Convoy.
9. 19 May: Howe discovers Brest Fleet has sailed.
10. Battle on 28 May.
11. Battle on 29 May.
12. 29 May: Caryfort encounters and captures *Castor*.
13. Battle on 1 June.
14. 8–9 June: Montagu's Squadron encounters Cornic Squadron and Brest Fleet.
15. 12 June: Grain Convoy arrives off Brest.
16. 13 June: Channel Fleet arrives at Portsmouth.

INTRODUCTION

As 1794 opened, Revolutionary France stood on the knife-edge of failure. Its army and navy had been shaken by the revolution. Both services had replaced the aristocrats which provided most officers with commoners. These new officers had proper revolutionary zeal, but often lacked requisite leadership knowledge and skills. France was at war with most of Europe. Britain, the Netherlands, Austria and Prussia were attacking Revolutionary France. Even Spain, France's traditional ally, had joined the anti-revolutionary coalition. Counter-revolutions which erupted in the Vendée and at Toulon in 1793 had been crushed before the new year dawned, but fresh unrest waited to erupt.

Worse, famine stalked the land. Crops had failed in 1793. The turmoil caused by the Revolution left many fields untilled. Poor weather led to meagre harvests in the few fields planted in 1793. Even if the First Republic government played the game of supplying loyal areas with food denied to restive provinces, there was too little food to go around.

Food was available. France's Caribbean holdings were still uncaptured. They produced sugar and rice. The new United States had plenty of surplus grain. Individual ships could smuggle in food, despite the British blockade, porous at this early stage of the war. The Committee of Public Safety, France's national government in 1794, wanted a reserve built up; something to assure its people food was available. It decided to organize a massive convoy to bring the New World's bounty to France.

It would be a gamble. The convoy would exceed 100 merchant vessels. It could assemble in safety in Chesapeake Bay. The anchorage was sheltered; within the territorial waters of the neutral United States. Britain was unwilling to risk war with the United States by violating these territorial waters to seize the French merchantmen. Once assembled, it still needed to reach France. It could only do that by crossing the North Atlantic, an ocean patrolled by the Royal Navy.

At the start of the Wars of French Revolution naval power was measured by ships-of-the-line. These were ships with square sails on all three masts armed with at least two complete decks of guns, and additional guns on the forecastle and

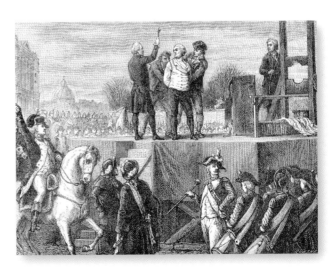

The execution of King Louis XVI by the French revolutionary government on 21 January 1793 precipitated a general war in Europe, involving Great Britain, the Dutch Republic and Spain in a coalition against France. (AC)

quarterdeck. The biggest ships-of-the-line had three gun decks. A warship was not considered a ship-of-the-line unless it was sturdy enough to take its place in the line of battle, a formation where the ships formed a line end to end. Ships mounting fewer than 64 long guns were considered too weak to trade broadsides in a line of battle, even when they had two complete gun decks.

In 1794 the Royal Navy was the world's most powerful navy. The Royal Navy began 1794 with 117 ships-of-the-line capable of taking to sea (including two captured from France), and 122 seagoing frigates (used for scouting and commerce raiding). Of these, 85 ships-of-the-line and 102 frigates were in commission, armed, manned and ready to fight. France's Marine Nationale began the war with 86 ships-of-the-line and 78 frigates, including those under construction. During 1793 France lost 15 ships-of-the-line and 18 frigates. Of the remaining warships, perhaps two-thirds were capable of going to sea.

The situation France faced was mitigated somewhat because Britain had to scatter its fleet around the world, while France's remaining warships were concentrated in its Atlantic naval harbours: Brest, Lorient and Rochefort. Yet the British stationed a formidable percentage of their ships-of-the-line in their Channel Fleet, assigned to keep watch over Brest.

The French government decided to gamble. It sent a force of ships-of-the-line and frigates to America. This escort was capable of overpowering a marauding frigate or privateer, or any likely combination of cruisers. These ships would bring the convoy to France. Then, to ensure the convoy could not be attacked by a squadron or fleet of ships-of-the-line, the convoy's approach would be covered by a sortie of the Brest Fleet and the Rochefort Squadron with over 30 of France's remaining ships-of-the-line.

Britain realized the opportunity the convoy offered. The British government saw its capture as an opportunity to hurt Republican France. The officers of the Royal Navy saw the convoy as an opportunity for prize money, awarded for taking enemy vessels – naval or civilian. They also saw an opportunity for something else: the glory, fame and promotion which accompanied a victorious naval battle. France would almost certainly protect its convoy with its Atlantic fleets. When France sent its fleet to sea, it offered Britain an opportunity to fight and win a naval battle. In British eyes, any naval battle could have only one outcome: a British victory.

The stage was set for a unique naval campaign. It was one fought over the course of a month. It saw the only fleet action during the French Revolutionary or Napoleonic Wars fought over multiple days, a series of actions stretching over nearly a week. It saw the only fleet action during the Age of Fighting Sail fought in the open ocean, hundreds of miles from shore. There would be no cape, bank or headland to name the battles after. Instead they would be named for the date on which they were fought. To the French, the final day's battle, the decisive date when they lost seven ships-of-the-line was called 'la Bataille du 13 prairial', for the day in their new, scientific Revolutionary calendar. The British also called the battle by the date on their calendar, prefixing it with a descriptive adjective. To them it was not the Battle of the First of June. It became known as the Glorious First of June.

The Marine Nationale was riven by politics in 1793. Within the arsenal at Brest, sailors became political activists, and fidelity to the revolution became more important than naval competence. (AC)

It was the only naval campaign fought during the French Revolutionary or Napoleonic Wars with the potential to have ended the French Revolution. Had Britain captured the grain convoy, it might have forced the surrender of Republican France. By New Year's Day, 1795, French monarchy would have been restored with the House of Bourbon once more ruling France. The roll of British naval and French land victories so famous today would not have taken place. St Vincent, Camperdown, Trafalgar, Marengo, Austerlitz, Eylau – even Leipzig and Waterloo – would have remained simple geographic descriptions.

Howe's flagship, *Queen Charlotte*, exchanges broadsides with *Montagne* after breaking the French line. (AC)

CHRONOLOGY

1789

5 May — The Estates General convenes in Versailles, starting the French Revolution.

1791

20 June — Louis XVI and family flee the palace. They are recaptured the next day and imprisoned in Paris.

1792

20 April — France declares war on Austria. (Prussia soon allies with Austria.)

10 August — Tuileries Palace stormed by the National Guard of the Paris Commune, causing the fall of the monarchy.

22 September — French Republic is established, the Marine Royale (Royal Navy) becomes the Marine Nationale (National Navy).

1 December — The Royal Navy begins recruiting as the navy goes onto a war footing.

1793

21 January — Louis XVI executed, Britain expels the French ambassador.

1 February — France declares war on Great Britain and the Netherlands.

7 March — France declares war on Spain, Portugal enters the war as a Spanish ally.

June — Jean Bon Saint-André joins the Committee of Public Safety and is given responsibility for the Marine Nationale.

29 August — Capture of Toulon by the Allies.

September — Jean Bon Saint-André purges the Brest Fleet of 'counter-revolutionary' officers, replacing them with politically reliable officers.

Autumn — Crop failure in France, especially in Brittany and the French maritime provinces.

19 December — Recapture of Toulon by France.

26 December — Rear Admiral Pierre Jean Van Stabel's Squadron leaves Brest bound for the United States to serve as escort for a food convoy.

1794

January — Tricolour adopted as French national flag.

January — Louis-Thomas Villaret de Joyeuse promoted to rear admiral and given command of the Brest Fleet.

11 February — Van Stabel's Squadron arrives in Norfolk, Virginia.

10 April — Rear Admiral Joseph-Marie Nielly departs Rochefort with a squadron of five ships-of-the-line and several frigates and corvettes with orders to rendezvous with Van Stabel.

11 April — Atlantic convoy, between 117 and 170 sail escorted by Vastabel's warships, departs Chesapeake Bay for France.

2 May — Channel Fleet, along with 99 merchant ships being convoyed to the East Indies and their warship escort, sail from Spithead.

7 May — *Atalante* captured by HMS *Swiftsure*.

9 May — *Sans Pareil* captures HMS *Castor* escorting a Newfoundland convoy of 30 sail.

11 May	The East Indies convoy reaches the latitude of Cape Finisterre. Admiral Montagu's squadron detaches from the convoy to seek out the French grain convoy.	**30 May**	Montagu's squadron arrives at Plymouth.
15 May	Admiral Montagu's squadron captures Marine Nationale corvette *Maire-Guiton* and recaptures ten merchant vessels captured earlier from the Newfoundland Convoy.	**1 June**	General fleet action occurs between Brest Fleet and Channel Fleet. Six Marine Nationale ships-of-the-line captured, one sunk.
		3 June	The Channel Fleet starts its return to port.
16 May	Brest Fleet, commanded by Rear Admiral Louis-Thomas Villaret-Joyeuse sails from Brest.	**4 June**	Montagu's squadron departs Plymouth for Brest.
17 May	The Channel Fleet and Brest Fleet pass each other in the fog without detecting the presence of the other fleet.	**8 June**	Montagu's squadron chases Cornic's squadron into Brest.
19 May	Howe discovers the French Fleet has left Brest.	**9 June**	The Brest Fleet arrives off Ushant, chasing off Montagu.
	Villaret-Joyeuse and the Brest Fleet encounter a Dutch convoy with 53 merchant ships and a two-warship escort sailing to Lisbon, and capture 18 to 20 merchantmen.	**11 June**	The Brest Fleet arrives at the Bertheaume Roads, outside Brest.
		12 June	The Grain Convoy arrives at the Raz de Sein, the southern passage to Brest.
20 May	Channel Fleet recaptures ten merchant vessels taken earlier from the Lisbon Convoy.	**13 June**	The Channel Fleet arrives at Portsmouth.
25 May	Channel Fleet encounters Marine Nationale ship-of-the-line *Audacieux*, two corvettes and a captured merchant brig, capturing both corvettes and the prize.	**14 June**	The Brest Fleet and Grain Convoy enter Brest Harbour.
		26 June	George III visits the Channel Fleet at Portsmouth.
28 May	Contact made with the Brest Fleet, with fighting occurring between the British Flying Squadron and rear elements of the French Fleet.		
29 May	A battle is fought between Brest Fleet and Channel Fleet which ends inconclusively at nightfall.		
	Caryfort encounters and captures *Castor* after a 90-minute frigate duel.		

OPPOSING COMMANDERS

High naval command demanded competence and courage. The sea implacably enforced high standards of competence on those travelling on it. Incompetent captains tended to remove themselves from candidates for promotion to flag rank. They made a fatal mistake in combat during a century in which naval wars marked every decade. Failing that, they fell foul of the hazards of the sea. Shipwreck and storm did not respect birth or privilege.

Command at sea also required physical courage. Captains and admirals conducted their activities from the quarterdeck. It was the highest deck, open to the elements. It afforded the best view of activities aboard a ship, and the best view of the sea immediately surrounding a ship available without going aloft into the rigging. It gave a commanding officer the situational awareness necessary to conduct a battle.

Richard Howe was the senior admiral of the Royal Navy when the battle was fought, Admiral of the Fleet. While other admirals marked their flagships with a red, white, or blue ensign at the appropriate mast, as Admiral of the Fleet Howe flew a Union Jack at the mainmast mast top. (AC)

It was also the most exposed position on a warship. If a captain or admiral could see everything, everyone else could see him. Officers wore distinctive uniforms, and killing a ship's commanders was a good way to throw a ship into disorder. Marksmen aboard enemy ships targeted officers. Even outside musket range, artillery aimed at the quarterdeck. Because commanders directed the ship, cowardice was quickly exposed, including when a ship mysteriously proved unable to engage the enemy even though the rest of the fleet present could.

Admirals were typically chosen from the most senior (and presumably most experienced) captains. While this usually meant an admiral would be a competent sailor and personally courageous, it did not mean the admiral would be imaginative or brilliant, especially after a decade of peace. Combat was required to reveal those traits. Indeed, admirals tended to be conservative, a lifetime of battling the ocean and its hazards enforcing the belief that you cannot be too careful.

There were three admirals' ranks, in order of increasing seniority: rear admiral, vice admiral and admiral. Traditionally, fleets were divided into three divisions: a vice admiral commanding the van (front); an admiral (in overall command of the fleet) directly commanding the centre; and a rear admiral in charge of the rear. In reality, fleet commands were assigned by seniority with the most senior admiral, whether a rear, vice or full admiral in charge of the fleet, the second most senior commanding the van, and the third most senior running the rear. Other, more junior admirals would be assigned squadrons for special duties. (In the Channel Fleet the four fastest ships-of-the-line were formed into a flying squadron used for scouting, under the command of a junior admiral.)

ROYAL NAVY COMMANDERS

In the 1790s the Royal Navy used merit (and influence) for promotion in the junior ranks: midshipman, lieutenant, commander and captain. After a man was promoted to captain, strict seniority reigned. He was junior to any captain who held that rank before him, and senior to any captain achieving that rank after him. As senior officers died, retired or were superannuated (involuntarily placed on the inactive list), he moved up the list of captains. Once at the top, promotion to admiral occurred automatically, with the next vacancy in the admirals list.

At 68 or 69 Richard Howe was the oldest admiral to command a fleet action when this campaign was fought. He had been in the Royal Navy over 55 years in 1794. (AC)

11

In the Royal Navy each admiral's rank was divided into three squadrons: blue, white and red. Blue marked the most junior third of the rear and vice admirals; red the most senior third. In 1793 there was only one admiral of the red, the most senior admiral, known as the admiral of the fleet. The remaining full admirals were divided evenly between the blue and white squadrons, with the senior half in the white squadron.

Admirals and commodores were known as flag officers, because they flew a flag at the peak of one of the masts of the ships that they commanded. In 1794 Royal Navy admirals flew their flag on the peak of the main mast, vice admirals on the fore mast and rear admirals on the mizzen (aft) mast. Commodores flew a swallow-tailed broad pennant. The different flag colours and locations allowed quick identification of the admirals' ships (or flagships) in an era with limited communications.

During the Atlantic Campaign of 1794, **Richard, Viscount Howe** commanded the Channel Fleet. He was then the senior admiral in the Royal Navy, the only man entitled to fly the Union Jack from the peak of the mainmast.

He was born in March or April of 1725 or 1726, the second son of Emmanuel Scrope Howe, second Viscount Howe. His mother was the daughter of a royal favourite, and the Howes benefited from royal favour throughout his career. Richard Howe is believed to have been educated at Westminster and later at Eton.

He joined the navy in 1739, rising due to his own merits more than royal patronage. By 1794 he was participating in his fourth major worldwide conflict. In the War of Austrian Succession (1739–48), he took part in the Anson Expedition as a volunteer aboard *Severn*. By 1745 he was a lieutenant, commanding *Baltimore*, a 14-gun brig-sloop.

He was promoted to captain during the Jacobite uprising of 1745. By the end of the war Howe commanded the 80-gun three-decker *Cornwall*, as Admiral Knowles' flag-captain.

Howe remained employed at sea almost continuously between 1750 and 1755. Before the Seven Years War (1756–63) began, he was sent to North America as captain of *Dunkirk*. As part of Boscawen's fleet, Howe participated in the opening battle of the war. He became Viscount Howe when his older brother was killed at Ticonderoga. Later in the war he was promoted to commodore (a temporary rank) participating in raids and actions at Saint-Malo, Saint Cast, Cherbourg and Rochefort. He led the line-of-battle at the Battle of Quiberon Bay in 1759.

In April 1763 he was appointed the First Sea Lord on the Board of Admiralty, serving until July 1765, when he was named Treasurer of the Navy. He remained there until 1770 when promoted to rear admiral and given command of the Mediterranean Fleet. Rising to vice admiral in February 1776, he was named commander-in-chief of the North American Station, despite his sympathies towards the colonial rebels.

Howe resigned this command in September 1778, citing a lack of proper support by Parliament. He entered Parliament in opposition to the North government, remaining ashore until the North government fell in April 1782. He then took command of the Channel Fleet, was promoted to admiral, and made a British viscount (his previous title had been in the Irish peerage) that same month. Over the next year he successfully accomplished several difficult tasks: he contained the Dutch fleet in Texel; protected a critical West Indies convoy from a Franco–Spanish fleet nearly 50 per cent larger than his; and relieved Gibraltar, then under siege by the Spanish.

He became First Lord of the Admiralty in January 1783, serving as head of the

Alexander Hood was the younger brother of Samuel Hood, then commanding the Mediterranean Fleet. Alexander, third in command of the Channel Fleet at the First of June, became its commander in 1795 with the retirement of Howe and Graves. (AC)

ALEXANDER HOOD.
VISCOUNT BRIDPORT

Royal Navy until 1788. Elevated to an earl when he left, he again assumed command of the Channel Fleet during the 1790 Spanish Armament. When the French Revolutionary Wars started in 1793, King George III once more gave Howe command of the Channel Fleet, which he commanded during this campaign.

Vice Admiral (red) Thomas Graves was Howe's second-in-command while Howe commanded the Channel Fleet. Graves commanded the van division during the battles fought between 28 May and 1 June.

Born on 23 October 1725, the second son of Rear Admiral Thomas Graves, Thomas Graves entered the Royal Navy at an early age, taking part in the 1741 Cartagena expedition aboard *Norfolk* at the age of 16. Promoted to lieutenant in June 1743, Graves fought at three major fleet actions during the War of the Austrian Succession. He was promoted to command of the sloop-of-war *Hazard* in 1754, and the frigate *Sheerness* in 1755.

Early in the Seven Years War Graves was court-martialled and reprimanded for failing to engage a French ship. This did not hurt his career. He was promoted to *Unicorn* (a 28-gun frigate) in 1758, given temporary command of the 50-gun *Oxford* in 1761, and appointed to *Antelope* (50) in 1762.

He remained employed in various postings between the Seven Years War and American Revolution. In 1778, commanding *Conqueror* (74) he was sent to the North American Station. Recalled in 1779 he was promoted to rear admiral in March 1779, becoming commander-in-chief of the North American Station in 1781. He commanded the British fleet at the Battle of the Chesapeake (a rare British defeat), and commanded a squadron of ships damaged and captured at the Battle of the Saintes to England. Caught by a hurricane, six ships-of-the-line sank (including the one Graves was aboard).

Promoted to vice admiral in 1787, Graves was named Howe's principal subordinate when war with France started in 1793. Badly injured during the battle fought on 1 June, he never held active command again. He was promoted to admiral and created the 1st Baron Graves in recognition of his service.

Vice Admiral (red) Sir Alexander Hood was Howe's third-in-command during the period leading to and including this campaign. During the three battles he commanded the rear division aboard *Royal George*.

He was born in 1726, the younger brother of Samuel Hood. Alexander Hood joined the Royal Navy as captain's servant aboard *Romney* in 1740 or 1741. In May 1743 he was appointed a midshipman aboard *Princess Mary*. After several other assignments, he was promoted to lieutenant in December 1746 aboard *Bridgewater* (20). After a stint on half-pay between 1748 and 1755, he was appointed lieutenant aboard *Prince* (80). Given command of *Merlin* (10) in March 1756, that June he was promoted captain, and appointed flag captain of *Prince George* (80) under Admiral Charles Saunders.

Hood remained Saunders' flag captain on four different ships through June 1759, when Hood gained command of the frigate *Minerva*. In 1763 he was given command of *Katherine*, a royal yacht.

In 1777 Hood left *Katherine* for *Robust* (74) as the American Revolution began. Present at the Battle of Ushant, he testified for Admiral

Keppel, but was found to have altered his log book after the battle. Hood left *Robust* after the court martial, resuming command of *Katherine*. Hood was promoted to rear admiral in September 1780, and appointed to a command subordinate to Lord Howe in the Grand Fleet in 1782. He was elected to Parliament in 1784, promoted to vice admiral and made a knight of the Bath in 1787. In February 1793 he was appointed to the Channel Fleet under Howe again.

For services during the battles he was elevated to Lord Bridport, an Irish peerage. With Graves' retirement he became second-in-command-of-the Channel Fleet after the battle, assuming command of it in 1795. He retired from that command in 1800.

MARINE NATIONALE COMMANDERS

To say the senior officer corps of Revolutionary France's Marine Nationale were less tradition bound than their Royal Navy counterparts would be an understatement. In some

Louis Thomas Villaret de Joyeuse was probably the best choice for Republican France to command the Brest Fleet. Although an ardent republican, Villaret-Joyeuse was a competent seaman who had served many years. With better political connections while in the Marine Royale, Villaret-Joyeuse would have been at least a captain, and possibly an admiral. (AC)

ways, the Marine Nationale was 150 years ahead of its time. Its admirals were picked primarily for political reliability rather than leadership skills or maritime competence, an innovation not imitated until the 20th century. It even incorporated a concept other navies would not use until the 20th century: political officers. Even admirals had representatives of the Committee for Public Safety (then France's de facto ruling body) aboard their flagships, monitoring their behaviour.

Navies tend to be conservative and competent, never more so than in the Age of Sail. Travelling by sea was dangerous. The incompetent quickly died, often taking others with them. The result was an organization which went with what worked in the past, accepting change only when it proved clearly superior to past practice. This predisposition towards conservatism was magnified in the Marine Royale of the *Ancien Régime*, which limited the officer corps to the nobility.

The combination of departure from the navy by aristocratic officers fleeing France, purges of admirals demonstrating counter-revolutionary behaviour, and officer-led naval mutinies in support of the monarchy at Toulon and Brest 1793 created opportunities for the revolutionarily-minded to advance. In 1793 the Committee for Public Safety replaced most aristocratic officers with supporters of the revolution. Promoted were officers already in the Marine Nationale and officers from France's merchant marine. This resulted in very

Jean Bon Saint-André was a failed merchant captain who became a politician when the French Revolution started. Although he knew nothing of naval affairs, he parlayed his commercial maritime experience into a position as the governing committee's naval expert. Many of his actions weakened the Marine Nationale. (AC)

junior officers, including those who had been ensigns or lieutenants prior to 1791, being advanced to flag rank. Many proved surprisingly competent. The leaders in Marine Nationale during this campaign included:

Contre-Amiral (Rear Admiral) Louis Thomas Villaret de Joyeuse was born at Auch, Languedoc, on 29 May 1747. He came from a noble family, joining the King's guard in his teens, most likely as a member of the Gardes-du-Corps du Roi. He transferred to the navy after killing a comrade in a duel. In 1773, he was assigned to the frigate *Atalante* (32), sent to Indian waters.

Villaret-Joyeuse served in the Indies throughout the Wars of American Independence, under the command of Suffren, France's most brilliant admiral. Villaret Joyeuse became Suffren's aide-de-camp in 1782, and later served as first lieutenant aboard *Brilliant* (64), and later commanded the frigate *Bellone* and corvette *Naiade*. He lost *Naiade* after an epic five-hour fight with a British 64-gun ship-of-the-line, was captured and freed in June 1783, after peace was signed. Despite these services, in 1784 Villaret-Joyeuse was only promoted to a permanent rank of senior lieutenant (*lieutenant de vaisseau*). Lacking influence, he remained a lieutenant until 1792.

Although an aristocrat, in March 1792 he swore allegiance to the Republican government. In June he was promoted to captain, and in 1793 he was given command of *Trajan* (74). When the Quiberon mutiny broke out in September 1793, Villaret-Joyeuse stayed loyal to the Republican government. When the mutiny collapsed, the Committee for Public Safety removed all officers suspected of Royalist sympathies. Villaret-Joyeuse was the most experienced and competent officer loyal to the revolution. In early 1794 he was promoted to rear admiral and given command of the Brest Fleet, commanding it during this campaign.

He retained command of the fleet until 1796, being promoted to vice admiral in September 1794. He was imprisoned in 1796 after being accused of Royalist sympathies, but restored to the navy after Napoleon took over. He supported the Bonaparte regime until his death in 1812.

Représentant en mission Jean Bon Saint-André accompanied the Brest fleet during this campaign aboard Villaret-Joyeuse's flagship *Montagne* as an extraordinary envoy of the National Convention. His official purpose was to report on the condition of the fleet during action. His real purpose was to monitor the behaviour of Villaret-Joyeuse, and ensure the fleet carried out its mission of protecting the grain convoy with sufficient revolutionary ardour.

Born on 25 February 1749 as Antoine Jeanbon, he was the son of a Protestant fuller from Montauban. He was educated by Jesuits and studied law, but was barred from that career because he came from a Protestant family. Instead he entered France's merchant marine, eventually becoming a merchant captain. He abandoned the sea after three shipwrecks, which left him penniless. He became a Huguenot pastor.

He supported the revolution and gained a seat in the Assembly. He joined the Montagne (Mountain) faction and became a member of the Committee for Public Safety. As their maritime expert he was given responsibility for the navy, which he reformed with an eye towards egalitarian behaviour. Among his reforms were the abolition of the navy's artillery corps (viewed as elitist), and the reformation of the officer corps. He designed the French Tricolour flag.

With the collapse of the Montagne faction, Saint André was removed from the Committee for Public Safety. Although arrested he avoided execution. Freed during the amnesty in 1795, he served in various diplomatic and

VANSTABEL.

One of the rare commoner officers in the Marine Royale, Pierre-Jean Van Stabel experienced a meteoric rise in the Marine Nationale, rising from a *lieutenant* to *contre-amiral* in just over a year. (AC)

administrative roles in Republican and Napoleonic France, until his death from typhus in 1813.

Contre-Amiral Pierre Jean Van Stabel commanded the close escort for the grain convoy from America, and shepherded the convoy from the Chesapeake to Brest.

Van Stabel was born on 8 November 1744 in Dunkirk. His family were merchant sailors, and he served aboard his first merchant vessel when he was 14. By the outbreak of the American Revolution he had risen to captain of a merchant vessel. He took command of a privateer, *Dunkerquoise* in 1778, and would command two others between 1781 and the end of the war. He was promoted to junior lieutenant (*lieutenant de frigate*) in the Marine Royale in 1782, remaining in the navy after the war ended. He conducted a hydrographic survey of the English Channel in 1788.

He remained in the navy during the Revolution. He was given command of the frigate *Proserpine* (36) in 1792, spending a year in the Caribbean. When war with England broke out in February 1793, he was promoted to captain. In November he was promoted to rear admiral. He distinguished himself in a week-long battle against a superior British fleet in which the ten ships he commanded managed to snatch 17 merchant ships from a convoy guarded by 28 Royal Navy warships, only losing one corvette in exchange.

He was sent to North America later that year, with the task of bringing a grain convoy safely to France, a task he successfully completed between April and June 1794. He later commanded a squadron operating in the English Channel and North Sea, but died in Dunkirk in March 1797.

During this campaign **Contre-Amiral Joseph-Marie Nielly** commanded the Rochefort Squadron, initially sent to reinforce Van Stabel's convoy escort. As the campaign developed, he instead rendezvoused with the Brest Fleet, commanding the rear division in the battle fought on 1 June.

He was born in Brest in 1751, to a commoner family. He joined the Marine Royale at the age of seven, and was wounded at the 1759 Battle of Quiberon Bay in the Seven Years War. He remained in the navy until 1769, seeing service in the Caribbean. He remained at sea in the merchant service, rising to command of a merchantman in 1774. He rejoined the Marine Royale in 1778 with the start of French involvement in the American Revolution, at the rank of junior lieutenant. He commanded a 20-gun corvette during the war.

He returned to merchant service when the war ended, but rejoined the navy in 1787 again a junior lieutenant, when reforms permitted admission of non-noble officers during peacetime. In 1792, after war broke out, he was promoted to senior lieutenant, and then in January 1793 to senior captain (*capitaine de vaisseau*). He commanded the frigate *Résolue* in the Atlantic, Bay of Biscay, and the Channel. A staunch Republican, he was promoted to rear admiral in November 1793, and given command of the Rochefort Squadron soon after.

Following the Atlantic Campaign of May 1794, he remained with the Brest Fleet, commanding squadrons and seeing action at the Action of 6 November 1794, and the 1796 attempt to invade Ireland. Later he served as the port commander at Brest and Lorient, Maritime Prefect at Dunkirk. He retired in 1803, and died in Brest in 1833.

OPPOSING NAVIES

Through the lens of time the two navies opposing each other in this campaign, the Royal Navy of Great Britain and the Marine Nationale of Revolutionary France, appear more similar than different. Both sides used the same types of warships: wooden sailing ships armed with rows of smoothbore cannon. Both sides used similar manning structures for their vessels, with crews divided into officers, warrant officers, petty officers and sailors. The names were different, but the meanings identical. Both sides used similar tactics, fighting battles with ships in line-ahead formation, trading broadsides.

There were five major categories of warships in 1794: ships-of-the-line, two-deckers, frigates, sloops-of-war (or corvettes) and dispatch vessels.

The biggest were ships-of-the line. These were full-rigged ships, with three masts, all carrying square sails. These were vessels powerful enough to sail in the line of battle. All mounted at least 64 guns on at least two full gun decks, with additional guns mounted on the forecastle and quarterdeck. The largest had three full gun decks with up to 120 guns. Most mounted smoothbore, muzzle-loading cannon which fired balls weighing between 32 to 42 pounds on the lower deck, with 24-pdr or 18-pdr cannon on the upper gun decks. The quarterdeck and forecastles, raised partial decks at the stern and bow, mounted guns which fired four-pound to nine-pound shot. By 1794 the standard ship-of-the-line was the two-deck 74, with 64s considered on the light side. Ships-of-the-line were commanded by senior captains.

Both navies used the same types of warships: the ship-of-the-line (centre), frigate (right) and corvette or sloop-of-war (left). Ships-of-the-line and frigates were full-rigged ships. Corvettes had a bewildering variety of rigs, including the lugger rig of this illustration. (AC)

Operating a warship required skilled sailors, proficient in the duties of their trade. Warships attempted to keep a mix of one-third able seamen (highly skilled), one-third ordinary seamen (proficient) and one-third landsmen (unskilled beginners). These men are typical of those who served aboard British warships in 1794. (AC)

The frigate was a full-rigged ship, with one full gun deck and guns mounted on the forecastle and quarterdeck. The largest frigates mounted 40 to 44 guns, the lightest 28 to 32 guns. The standard frigate of the era mounted 36 or 38 guns. Main deck guns ranged from 9-pdrs to 24-pdrs, with the 12-pound gun standard for light frigates and 18-pounders for heavy frigates. Frigates were used for commerce raiding, convoy protection, or – when attached to a fleet of ships-of-the-line – scouting. Frigates were typically commanded by junior captains.

Sloops-of-war (called corvettes in the Marine Nationale) were single-decked warships mounting between eight and 24 guns. Most only carried guns on the gun deck. A few were large enough to mount guns on their quarterdecks. Smaller than frigates, these vessels were used in much the same role, albeit with less capability. The largest vessels were full-rigged ships, although many used different square-rigged two-mast rigs: brig, brigantine, and ketch. They were commanded by commanders, lieutenant-commanders or sometimes lieutenants, although the commanders always carried the courtesy title 'captain'.

Dispatch vessels were the smallest warships; in some cases smaller than the largest ships' boats on three-deckers. These were used to carry messages and mail. Most carried between four to eight guns, generally of the lightest size. They depended on speed for safety, and were commanded by lieutenants or even masters (a warrant rank).

The ships were so similar that when ships of one side were captured by the other, the prize ships became part of the captor's navy. Sometimes, even the artillery was retained. (In this campaign one warship was captured by the French, commissioned in the Marine Nationale, and then captured by the British, and recommissioned as a Royal Navy warship, all within one month.)

Yet the two navies were different in ways that were more important than their apparent similarities. One navy was primarily a volunteer service, while the other was a conscript navy. One was a meritocracy, while in the other promotion was gained through political favour. One had an efficient administration, while the other was handicapped by an inefficient bureaucracy. One was manned by experienced officers and skilled seamen who worked as a team. The other had officers appointed at whim, lacked a core of experienced mariners and rarely trained as a team.

Ironically, monarchical Britain, with its class system and a long-standing organizational bureaucracy had the meritocratic, volunteer navy with efficient administration and long-standing crews. Egalitarian France had a conscript navy with officers appointed by political committee, an inefficient (and sometimes corrupt) administration, and ill-trained, short-term crews. Ultimately, these differences proved more important than the similarities.

ROYAL NAVY

At the start of 1794 the Royal Navy had 85 ships-of-the-line in commission, 32 laid up or under repair, and ten being built. Over half of the ships-of-the-line in commission, 51, were 74-gun ships-of-the-line. Two were 80-gun two-deckers, 18 were 64-gun ships of the line, and 14 were three-deckers. Slightly over 40 ships-of-the-line, including seven three-deckers, were available in the North Atlantic or Channel waters.

In addition, the Royal Navy had 20 44-gun or 50-gun two-deckers in commission. Too small to stand in the line of battle, these ships were used to escort convoys or serve as flagships at overseas stations. Three of these would take part in the campaign, escorting an East Indies convoy.

As 1794 began, the Royal Navy had 88 frigates and 62 sloops-of-war in commission. Perhaps a third of these were stationed in North Atlantic waters or in the English Channel, where they could

participate if needed. Only ten frigates and six sloops were directly attached to the British fleets engaged in this campaign. The rest were cruisers or convoy escorts, although a few, such as the frigate *Castor*, became involuntarily enmeshed in the action over the course of the campaign while carrying out independent duties.

In 1794 only ten per cent of Royal Navy crews were made up of pressed men. Impressment was used to make up shortages of skilled seamen. Men conscripted in by a 'hot press' (impressing men off merchant ships) were typically rated able or ordinary seamen. (AC)

While British warships of the era were considered less well designed than their French counterparts, by the 1790s this was no longer true. During the middle third of the 18th century Britain had adopted the best features of French naval architecture. In some cases, such as the British 38-gun frigates with an 18-pdr main battery, Britain had surpassed the French. Similarly, the newest British ships-of-the-line were equal or superior to the French vessels then being built.

Even when French warships could theoretically sail faster than their British equivalents, in practice the British warships were usually faster. French advantages in hull form could not compensate for British superiority in both masts and seamanship. The masts available to the British were superior to those available in France. This meant British warships could carry more sail (and get more thrust) than French warships. Their well-drilled crews could also get better performance out of their ships. It was a rare French warship that could outrun a British warship when chased; it was a rare British warship that could not outrun a French ship when flight was called for.

British ships-of-the-line typically mounted lighter long guns than their French opposites – 32-pdr long guns on the lower deck rather than the French 36-pdrs. However, the difference was often illusory. Starting in the American Revolution, the Royal Navy began supplementing the long guns with carronades. These were lightweight, short-barrelled smoothbores which could be mounted on upper decks which were too light to take even a 4-pdr long gun. They were short-ranged guns, but since British practice was to fight gunwale-to-gunwale, the short range mattered little. By 1794 most British ships-of-the-line mounted eight to 12 carronades capable of firing a 12- to 24-pound shot, typically adding another 100 pounds to a broadside.

In 1794 the Royal Navy was well-manned. It started in 1792 at its peacetime strength: 16,000 sailors and 4,000 marines. All of these men were volunteers; impressment, the Royal Navy's version of conscription, was used only during wartime. It virtually doubled this total in the last months of 1792, as war became imminent. As 1794 started, the navy had grown to an authorized strength of 73,000 sailors and 12,000 marines – an increase of over 400 per cent.

Despite this growth, the vast majority of the men in the Royal Navy in 1794 had joined willingly. Only around ten per cent of the ships' crews had been 'pressed,' or conscripted. The rest were volunteers, having enlisted in peacetime and been turned over to new ships, or voluntarily enlisted since the war started.

There were several reasons for this. Patriotism played a part. The events in Revolutionary France shocked most Englishmen, including many of its mariners. Many were willing to defend their nation against what they viewed as revolutionary excesses. Pay was another reason. During peacetime, merchant sailors' pay was equivalent to those in the navy. Wartime shortages of trained sailors caused merchant pay to skyrocket during wartime, but by 1794 merchant wages had not risen appreciably. Plus, you were certain to be paid if serving in the navy. Merchant wages were often uncertain.

Finally, working conditions on a naval ship were easier than on a merchantman. The heavy manpower requirements aboard naval ships (required to handle the guns, only used in battle) meant more sailors available for sail handling and other routine maritime activities. Discipline on a warship was no harsher, and often less arbitrary than that of merchant vessels.

Nor was impressment used to fill the ranks of British warships with unskilled personnel. It was used to obtain skilled mariners. Where 40 per cent of the volunteers were landsmen, only 16 per cent of impressed men were landsmen. Nearly half of those impressed, 49 per cent, entered the navy rated as petty officer or able seamen. The rest entered as ordinary seamen.

Two-thirds of a Royal Navy warship's crew was made up of seamen – men who manned the guns, tended the sails, handled the anchor, and did the everyday tasks associated with handling a ship. An additional sixth was made up of the ship's marine contingent, used to enforce discipline and serve as seaborne soldiers during battle. The remaining sixth was made up of the

A real strength of the Royal Navy was its series of naval ports and facilities, which kept the ships well supplied and maintained. This is Spithead, the anchorage outside Portsmouth, the Royal Navy's biggest port. (USNHHC)

officers – commissioned, warrant and petty – and specialists (known as idlers because they did not stand watch and normally worked only during daytime) with skills needed to keep a ship running, such as the armourer, carpenters and coopers' mates.

Of the seamen, the Royal Navy aimed at a mix of one-third landsmen (those with little or no previous experience at sea), one-third ordinary seamen (with three to six years' experience) and one-third able seamen (with six or more years' experience). The able seamen were men who could handle (knew the ropes controlling the sails), reef (work aloft with the sails) and steer (set and keep a course with a ship's wheel or tiller). These men were also the pool from which the petty officers were drawn. The petty officers provided first-line leadership, comprising the various mates (gunner's mates, bosun's mates) and 'captains' (captain of the maintop, captain of the hold, captain of the afterguard, etc.) needed to ensure smooth running of a ship.

The Royal Navy never had problems finding enough landsmen. These ranks were typically filled by volunteers, young, usually single men wishing to learn a skilled trade, see the world outside their home village, and – in wartime – maybe get rich through prize money. The Royal Navy was always short of skilled mariners during wartime. Due to the vast expansion of the fleet in 1793 and 1794, there were critical shortages of petty officers. Most ships only had three-quarters to two-thirds of those positions filled in early 1794.

The commissioned and warrant officers were also skilled mariners. To receive a commission, an officer had to have at least six years' sea service. While interest – family influence – helped some, ultimately every captain had to sleep sometimes. A ship had too few officers to allow a captain to sleep soundly with even one inept lieutenant. Survival dictated having a competent wardroom. The warrant officers were men of long experience in some critical aspect of seafaring: navigation, medicine, logistics or ship maintenance. They held warrants issued by boards which weeded out bunglers.

Regardless of rank, except for the geriatric admirals commanding the fleet, service in the Royal Navy of 1794 was a young man's game. Two-thirds of the lower deck were under the age of 30, with over half of the landsmen and ordinary sailors younger than 25.

The British sailors of 1794 were also largely from the British Isles. Over half, 51 per cent, were from England, 19 per cent Irish, 10 per cent Scots and 3 per cent Welsh. The nationality of the remaining sixth were either foreign or unknown. The lads who to glory did steer were British, and indeed freemen, not slaves.

MARINE NATIONALE

While the Royal Navy was ready and steady, in 1794 the Marine Nationale was in disarray.

The Marine Royale had almost been destroyed during the Seven Years War. A rebuilding period followed and it had finished the Wars of American Revolution in perhaps the best shape it would ever achieve. Following that war, the naval minister had embarked on an ambitious construction programme, building ships more powerful than their British counterparts. A major reform of the service was undertaken. A corps of naval gunners was established, and pay and service periods were revised. Officer ranks, formerly filled only by aristocrats, were opened to commoners 'of the better sort'.

Naval harbours improved, and the ships re-distributed. Over half the fleet was stationed at Brest, with the remaining ships split between Rochefort and Toulon. By the eve of the French Revolution the Marine Royale had 84 ships-of-the-line available and another 15 nearing completion, with over 70 frigates available. It was a navy that could have met the Royal Navy on nearly equal terms. All this changed in the five years between 5 May 1789, when the Estates General convened to start the French Revolution and 5 May 1794, when Admiral Nielly took the Rochefort Squadron to sea.

One change was the name. With the death of the king and the abolition of the monarchy, the Marine Royale became the Marine Nationale – the national navy instead of the king's navy. It had also shrunk significantly, both in terms of personnel and ships.

The most dramatic change was in the officer corps. Prior to the American Revolution, officers were exclusively drawn from the minor nobility. These were also typically the poorer aristocrats, possessing little other than their genealogy and aristocratic privileges. (Richer aristocrats managed their estates, served in the civil government or belonged to the army. Sea service was dangerous and uncomfortable.) Even after the Marine Royale began giving commoners commissions during the Wars of American Revolution, commoner officers were a minority and limited to the lower ranks of commissioned officers. Few rose as high as *lieutenant de vasseau*, and none higher.

When the revolutionary government abolished titles and aristocratic privileges, they stripped the vast majority of the Marine Nationale's officers of their most valuable possession. The results were predictable. Between 1790 when the nobility was abolished and 1793 when France declared war on

The French sailor (or matelot) was as skilled a mariner as his British counterpart. However, France had far fewer mariners, requiring more unskilled landsmen in warship crews. They also spent less time at sea, reducing sea experience. They were tough and tenacious fighters. (AC)

Britain, many aristocratic officers resigned, often emigrating with whatever resources they could take. Those that remained were often hostile to the new regime.

The attitude of the common sailor was just the opposite. The Marine Royale and later Marine Nationale conscripted sailors, using the *Inscription marine*. All Frenchmen who served in a maritime profession for at least a year were to register on the *rôle des gens de mer* (roll of mariners) at age 18, and annually thereafter. During peacetime, the sailor drafted tended to be the ne'er-do-well riff-raff that inhabited seaports, men who could not otherwise find employment. Married men and those belonging to maritime families were generally kept on the reserve rolls, called up during wartime.

Revolutionary efforts to impose equality in a ship's crew was supposed to create scenes like this one, with sailors and officers living together amicably. Instead, they shredded discipline, and reduced efficiency. (AC)

The result was a collapse of discipline that accelerated between 1791 and 1793. The sailors demanded equality, brotherhood and liberty, while the officers attempted to run the ships along traditional lines. Tradition viewed captains as masters under God in a nation that had abolished God along with the nobility. The ports became hotbeds of revolutionary fervour; admirals were humiliated, imprisoned and even lynched. Finally the officer corps was abolished and a new set of officers commissioned. Egalitarian rules were imposed (captains had to eat the same food as the crew, and were stripped of privileges of rank), and merchant captains with five years sea time could enter the Marine Nationale as officers.

In October 1793 Jean Bon Saint André issued a decree of purification. Lists of officers were posted. Anyone could denounce an officer for a lack of devotion to the revolution. Many did, often anonymously, sending the

The core of the Royal Navy's line of battle was the 74-gun ship-of-the-line. *Bellerophon*, which fought in this campaign, became one of the period's most famous 74s, eventually accepting Napoleon's surrender in 1815. (LOC)

" BARFLEUR," 98 GUNS, 1768
SHOWING STEERING WHEEL

HMS *Barfleur*, a model of which is shown, was launched in 1757. It was typical of the Royal Navy's small 90-gun three-deckers which actually had a lighter broadside than French 74-gun ships-of-the-line. (AC)

A model of a Téméraire-class 74-gun ship of the line. Designed by the French naval architect Jacques-Noël Sané, these ships formed the backbone of the Marine Nationale. Eight Téméraire-class ships participated in this campaign. (Rama)

accused before tribunals who believed it better to err favouring revolutionary fervour than facts. The resulting vacancies were often filled by those with the greatest revolutionary fervour rather than the greatest competence for their role.

Additionally the corps of naval-gunners was abolished at this time, also on egalitarian grounds at Saint André's insistence. His maritime experience was limited to merchant service, and he was unacquainted with the difficulties associated with operating artillery from a moving platform. He argued the corps was an aristocracy of the lower deck, and that any sailor could operate the guns.

The fleet was also affected by combat losses. France lost 15 ships-of-the-line and 18 frigates in 1793. All of the ships of the line lost were in the Mediterranean, which did not affect the strength of France's Atlantic squadrons, but five of the frigates lost had been in Atlantic waters. A more serious problem was that many of the naval stores that filled the naval harbours at Brest and Rochefort in 1789 had disappeared or degraded to uselessness by 1794. Those fleets faced shortages of masts, spars, cordage and sailcloth. Properly preserved and fresh food was also scarce. In 1793, ships in Brest Harbour experienced outbreaks of scurvy among their crews.

Yet while problems within the Atlantic squadrons participating in this campaign existed, they did not cripple the fleet. Incompetents had been promoted to positions of authority, but many of the new captains and

admirals were men of long experience who should have risen to those ranks except for the absence of influence or the misfortune of being born common. The worst rabble-rousers were being weeded out, and the fleet contained a core of competent, professional sailors aboard the ships. Additionally, many were motivated by revolutionary zeal. While revolutionary zeal did not improve seamanship or artillery accuracy, it did create a willingness to fight, even against long odds. The French might not handle their ships or their guns as well as the British, but they were willing to fight just as hard, or perhaps harder.

Launched in 1766, and sunk at the First of June, *Vengeur de Peuple* was one of the oldest French ships-of-the-line at the battle. It had been launched with the name *Marseillois*. (Rama)

ORDERS OF BATTLE

BRITISH NAVAL FORCES

Channel Fleet (directly under command of Lord Howe)

Ship	Rate	Captain	Admiral	Flag Captain
Queen Charlotte*[1,2,3]	1st Rate SOL (100)	Sir Andrew Snape Douglas	Richard, Earl Howe	Sir Roger Curtis (flag captain)
Royal George*[1,2,3]	1st Rate SOL (100)	William Domett	Sir Alexander Hood, KB	
Royal-Sovereign*[1,2,3]	1st Rate SOL (100)	Henry Nichols	Thomas Graves	
Barfleur*[1,2,3]	2nd rate SOL (90)	Cuthbert Collingwood	George Bowyer	
Impregnable*[1,2,3]	2nd rate SOL (90)	George Blagden Westcott	Benjamin Caldwell	
Queen*[1,2,3]	2nd rate SOL (90)	John Hutt	Alan Gardner	
Glory[1,2,3]	2nd rate SOL (90)	John Elphinstone		
Gibraltar[1,2,3]	3rd rate SOL (80)	Thomas Mackenzie		
Caesar[1,2,3]	3rd rate SOL (80)	Anthony Jason Pye Molloy		
Alfred[1,2,3]	3rd rate SOL (74)	John Bazely		
Audacious[1]	3rd rate SOL (74)	William Parker		
Bellerophon*[1,2,3]	3rd rate SOL (74)	William Hope	Thomas Pasley	
Brunswick[1,2,3]	3rd rate SOL (74)	John Harvey		
Culloden[1,2,3]	3rd rate SOL (74)	Isaac Schomberg		
Defence[1,2,3]	3rd rate SOL (74)	James Gambier		
Invincible[1,2,3]	3rd rate SOL (74)	Hon. Thomas Pakenham		
Leviathan[1,2,3]	3rd rate SOL (74)	Lord Hugh Seymour		
Majestic[1,2,3]	3rd rate SOL (74)	Charles Cotton		
Marlborough[1,2,3]	3rd rate SOL (74)	Hon. G. Cranfield Berkeley		
Montagu[1,2,3]	3rd rate SOL (74)	James Montagu		
Orion[1,2,3]	3rd rate SOL (74)	John Thomas Duckworth		
Ramillies[1,2,3]	3rd rate SOL (74)	Henry Harvey		
Russell[1,2,3]	3rd rate SOL (74)	John Willet Payne		
Thunderer[1,2,3]	3rd rate SOL (74)	Albemarle Bertie		
Tremendous[1,2,3]	3rd rate SOL (74)	James Pigott		
Valiant[1,2,3]	3rd rate SOL (74)	Thomas Pringle		
Latona[1,2,3]	Frigate (38)	Edward Thornborough		
Phaeton[1,2,3]	Frigate (38)	William Bentinck		
Aquilon[1,2,3]	Frigate (32)	Hon. Robert Stopford		
Niger[1,2,3]	Frigate (32)	Hon. Arthur Kaye Legge		

Ship	Type	Commander	
Southampton[1,2,3]	Frigate (32)	Hon. Robert Forbes	
Venus[1,2,3]	Frigate (32)	William Brown	
Pegasus[1,2,3]	Frigate (28)	Robert Barlow	
Charon[1,2,3]	Hospital Ship	George Countess	
Comet[1,2,3]	Fireship (14)	William Bradley	
Incendiary[1,2,3]	Fireship (14)	John Cook	
Kingfisher[1,2,3]	Sloop (18)	Thos. Le Marchant Gosselyn	
Ranger[1,2,3]	Cutter (10)	Charles Cotgrave	
Rattler[1,2,3]	Cutter (10)	John Winne	

Montagu's Squadron (detached 4 May)

Ship	Type	Commander	
Hector*	3rd rate SOL (74)	Lawrence Halstead	Rear Admiral George Montagu
Alexander	3rd rate SOL (74)	Richard Rodney Bligh	
Arrogant	3rd rate SOL (74)	Richard Lucas	
Bellona	3rd rate SOL (74)	George Wilson	
Ganges	3rd rate SOL (74)	William Truscott	
Theseus	3rd rate SOL (74)	Robert Calder	
Pallas	Frigate (32)	Henry Curzon	
Concorde	Frigate (36)	Sir Richard Strachan	

Attached to Montagu's Squadron, June 4

Ship	Type	Commander
Colossus	3rd rate SOL (74)	Charles Pole
Minotaur	3rd rate SOL (74)	Thomas Louis
Ruby	3rd rate SOL (64)	Sir Richard Bickerton

Convoys and Escorts

East Indies Convoy

Ship	Type	Commander
Suffolk	3rd rate SOL (74)	Peter Rainier
Sampson	3rd rate SOL (64)	Robert Montagu
Centurion	Two-decker (50)	Samuel Osborne
Argo	Two-decker (44)	William Clark
Resistance	Two-decker (44)	Edward Pakenham
Orpheus	Frigate (32)	Henry Newcome
Swift	Sloop (14)	

Plus 99 East Indiamen

Newfoundland Convoy

Ship	Type	Commander
Castor	Frigate (32)	Thomas Troubridge
plus 30	Merchant Ships	

Cork Convoy

Ship	Type	Commander
Swiftsure	3rd rate SOL (74)	Charles Boyles
St Albans	3rd rate SOL (64)	James Vashon

Plus an unknown number of sail

United Netherlands Naval Forces

Lisbon Convoy

Alliantie	Frigate (36)
Waakzaamheid	Sloop ((18)

Plus 53 merchant ships

REPUBLIC OF FRANCE NAVAL FORCES

Brest (later Grand) Fleet under the command of Villaret-Joyeuse, 16 May 1794

Ship	Type	Commander	
Montagne*[1,2,3]	1st Rate SOL (120)	Jean-Francois Vignot	Louis-Thomas Villaret-Joyeuse
Républicain*[1,2,3]	1st Rate SOL (110)	Pierre-Mandé Lebeau	Jean-François Bouvet
Révolutionnaire[1]	1st Rate SOL (110)	Vaudangel	
Terrible[1,2,3]	1st Rate SOL (110)	Pierre-Jacques Longer	
Indomptable[1,2,3]	2nd rate SOL (80)	Lamesle	
Jacobin[1,2,3]	2nd rate SOL (80)	Gassin	
Juste[1,2,3]	2nd rate SOL (80)	Blavet	
Scipion[1,2,3]	2nd rate SOL (80)	Huguet	
Achille[1,2,3]	3rd rate SOL (74)	Guillaume Jean Noel La Villegris	
America[1,2,3]	3rd rate SOL (74)	Louis L'Heritier	
Convention[1,2,3]	3rd rate SOL (74)	Joseph Allary	
Entreprenant[1,2,3]	3rd rate SOL (74)	Antoine Maximilien César Lefrancq	
Éole[1,2,3]	3rd rate SOL (74)	Bertrand Keranguen	
Gasparin[1,2,3]	3rd rate SOL (74)	Tardy	

Jemappes[1,2,3]	3rd rate SOL (74)	Desmartis	
Impétueux[1,2,3]	3rd rate SOL (74)	Pierre Douville	
Montagnard[1,2]	3rd rate SOL (74)	Jean-Baptiste-François Bompar	
Mont-Blanc[1,2]	3rd rate SOL (74)	Thévenard	
Mucius[1,2,3]	3rd rate SOL (74)	Lareguy	
Neptune[1,2,3]	3rd rate SOL (74)	Pierre Tiphaine	
Northumberland[1,2,3]	3rd rate SOL (74)	Jean Pierre Étienne	
Pelletier[1,2,3]	3rd rate SOL (74)	Berrade	
Tourville[1,2,3]	3rd rate SOL (74)	Langlois	
Tyrannicide[1,2,3]	3rd rate SOL (74)	Alain-Joseph Dordelin	
Vengeur du Peuple[1,2,3]	3rd rate SOL (74)	Renaudin-Jean François Renaudin	
Proserpine	Frigate (38)		
Bellone	Frigate (36)		
Galathée	Frigate (32)		
Gentille	Frigate (32)		
Précieuse	Frigate (32)		
Tamise	Frigate (32)	Jean-Marthe-Adrien L'Hermite	
Naïade	Corvette (16)		
Papillon	Corvette (12)		
Unite	Corvette (12)		

Plus two additional frigates and six additional corvettes whose names are unknown

Cornic Squadron (left at Brest)

*Majestueux**	1st Rate SOL (110)	unknown	Contre-Amiral Yves Cornic
Aquilon	3rd rate SOL (74)		
Jupiter	3rd rate SOL (74)		
Marat	3rd rate SOL (74)		
Nestor	3rd rate SOL (74)		
Redoubtable	3rd rate SOL (74)		
Revolution	3rd rate SOL (74)		
Superbe	3rd rate SOL (74)		
Either *Brutus* or *Hydra*	Frigate (44)		

Plus one frigate, one corvette, and one cutter, names unknown.

Van Stabel Squadron (from Brest, to guard grain convoy)

*Jean-Bart**	3rd rate SOL (74)	Pierre Jean Van Stabel	
Tigre	3rd rate SOL (74)		
Embuscade	frigate (32)		

Plus one additional frigate and brig-corvette, names unknown.

Independent Reinforcements (from Brest)

Trente-et-un Mai[3]	3rd rate SOL (74)	Honoré Ganteaume

Rochefort Squadron (Nielly)

*Sans Pareil**[3]	2nd rate SOL (80)	Jean-François Courand	Joseph-Marie Nielly
Audacieux[1]	3rd rate SOL (74)	Pilastre	
Patriote[1,2,3]	3rd rate SOL (74)	Lacadou	
Téméraire[3]	3rd rate SOL (74)	Morel	
Trajan[3]	3rd rate SOL (74)	Dumoutier	
Seine	Frigate (40)		
Atalante	Frigate (36)	Charles Linois	
Maire-Guiton	Corvette (20)		
Républicaine	Corvette (20)		
Inconnue	Brig-Corvette (16)		
Levrette	Brig-Corvette (16)		

Plus at least four more frigates and two corvettes whose names are unknown.

Notes

Only the composition of the fleets is given. Ships changed position in line of battle regularly. Data given in each row is rated number of guns, type of ship, ship's captain, flag officer aboard (if present). 'SOL' indicates the vessel is a ship-of-the-line.

Types of ships are:

1st rates carry 98 to 120 guns and have three full gun decks.

2nd rates carry 80 to 90 guns. British second rates have three full gun decks; French second rates have two gun decks.

3rd rates carry 64 to 80 guns. They have two full gun decks. Only British 80-gun ships are 3rd rates, French 80s are 2nd rates.

Two-decker, a ship with 40 to 50 guns on two full gun decks. These were considered too small to stand in the line of battle, although occasionally they did.

Frigates are ships carrying between 28 and 44 guns with one full gun deck and guns on the forecastle and quarterdeck.

Sloops and corvettes are ships carrying between 8 and 24 guns on one gun deck. Captains are listed if their names are known. Many French captains only have a last name known.

Markings following the name:

* – indicates a flagship

[1] – Present 28 May

[2] – Present 29 May

[3] – Present 1 June

OPPOSING PLANS

The year 1794 saw the two navies following two completely different strategies. In some ways it was like watching two football teams take the field playing by different sets of rules: one playing Association football, while the other followed the rules of American football. The result was each sought different objectives, both nations finished the campaign feeling they had won and the other nation had lost, and both – within the context of their objectives – were correct.

BRITISH PLANS

In 1794, the Royal Navy was comfortably superior to the Marine Nationale, even in the Atlantic. In 1790 and 1792 the Royal Navy had gone through mobilizations due to war scares with Spain and Russia. These had been settled without war, but the result was the Royal Navy entered the war against Revolutionary France well supplied and with their warships in good shape.

While Howe frequently complained about the status of his ships in 1793, no admiral was ever satisfied his ships were in good shape. He also had reservations about the aggressiveness and competence of some of his captains. It was something worth worrying over. Good peacetime captains often lacked qualities needed during wartime, and only combat revealed which captains had what it took to take a ship-of-the-line into close action.

Howe, commanding the Channel Fleet, knew the cost of a close blockade, especially in winter. It would wear out his line-of-battle vessels, stressing hulls, straining spars and masts, and rotting cordage and canvas. It also exhausted sailors, one commodity the Royal Navy was always short of and something Howe wished to husband.

Moreover, Howe did not really want to blockade the French fleet. He wanted it at sea, where it could be fought. Given the relative strengths of the opposing fleets and Britain's superiority, he wanted to fight and defeat it.

The stern of *Queen Charlotte*, Howe's flagship. The most powerful warship in the Royal Navy in 1793, it was a fitting command for the navy's senior admiral. (USNHHC)

Howe was following a policy developed and honed by the Royal Navy during the 18th century. When the Royal Navy had superiority over its foes, opportunities were sought to meet and defeat the enemy fleet, reducing its size through attrition. Simultaneously, the navy ensured freedom of movement for its merchant fleet and invading British armies, while protected Britain and its own colonies from invasion.

In 1794 Britain had an opportunity to exploit this strategy in a way that it had not since the Seven Years War, when the Royal Navy reduced the Marine Royale to impotence and then scooped up new colonies around the world. During the American Revolution, Britain had part of its fleet tied down monitoring the Colonial rebels when a coalition of France, Spain and the Netherlands, three formidable Continental maritime powers, entered the war. Britain fought that war on the defensive. But in 1794 France had no allies and the British knew the Marine Nationale was in disarray.

The key was seeking opportunities to find and fight the Brest fleet. Howe was less interested in keeping the French Atlantic fleet penned in port than he was in luring them into a battle. That could only happen if the French had an opportunity to *leave* port. Instead of close blockade, Howe had frigates monitoring Brest.

A fleet preparing for sea, especially a French fleet, gave plenty of advanced notice. Topmasts would have to be rigged, and spars crossed and sails bent before ships could sail. To prepare the French fleet for sea took weeks. While a watching frigate would have to go in close to be able to see if spars had canvas on them (which announced a ship about to sail), topmasts and spars could be clearly seen even at a distance.

Howe chose to keep the ships of his line of battle in port or at Tor Bay, an anchorage off Devon. From Tor Bay he was in a position to move against Brest if the French fleet showed signs of sailing, but was also close enough to the naval ports of Plymouth and Portsmouth for resupply and rest. This policy of relative inaction gained Howe criticism in Britain. He was mocked as 'Lord Torbay' by a public and press unaware of his strategy. The criticism indicated part of his plan was working. The French read British newspapers.

It is hard to lure an enemy out of port if they believe it to be a trap. Better for them to believe you were indolent.

Historians criticize Howe for his focus on the French navy, while neglecting the convoy. Yet modern economic warfare did not exist in 1794. While enemy merchant ships were legitimate targets, they were largely targets of opportunity. The system had emerged in an age when all ships, even cargo-carriers, were potential warships. Capturing captains saw them as a means of monetary reward (through prize money) rather than a way of starving an enemy nation.

Howe and his subordinate admirals had all begun their careers at sea two decades before Adam Smith's *Wealth of Nations* was published and introduced the modern concept of economics. It is hardly to be wondered their focus was on the enemy's fleet, rather than on the merchant fleet. Their view was that once the enemy's navy was dealt with, the merchant fleet would follow. Times were changing. Economic blockades such as those created by Napoleon's 1806 Berlin Decree or the retaliatory British 1807 Orders in Council emerged a decade later. That Howe had not anticipated this change is unsurprising.

FRENCH PLANS

France's strategy in this campaign was simple: get the grain convoy from North America to Brest safely. Everything else was subordinate to that, even the head of Villaret-Joyeux. He had been led to believe he would be executed if the grain convoy failed to arrive. This influenced his actions throughout this campaign.

The advantages of sending the grain in a convoy were twofold: it reduced the opportunity for the enemy to find the merchant vessels, and it also made it more difficult for the ships to be taken when found.

One of the chief advantages of the convoy system was that it concentrated ships in a small part of the ocean, making all of them harder to find, and making it difficult to capture more than one or two if it was found. (AC)

Convoys reduced the opportunity for ships to be found by concentrating potential prize ships in one location. Under normal conditions a lookout at the mast top of a sailing ship could spot another one ten to 15 nautical miles away. (Ten nautical miles was more typical in the North Atlantic.) The hull might be below the horizon (or hull down) but the masts and sails would

be above it and visible. If 100 merchant ships were sailing independently there would be 100 opportunities to come within sight of one of them. Collected together in a convoy those 100 ships offered just one opportunity for an enemy cruiser to encounter them.

A convoy would have a larger footprint than a single ship. Assuming the convoy was distributed in ten columns with ten rows, each 600 yards apart; an area roughly two nautical miles square. Instead of the 15-mile spotting distance of the single ship, the 100-ship convoy cut a swathe 17 miles in diameter. The actual footprint would be larger. There were always runners (ships that moved ahead of their position in the convoy) and stragglers (ships lagging behind the convoy). But a single oval perhaps 35 miles wide and 50 miles long was a lot harder to find than 100 30-mile diameter disks. The former covered 1,340 square miles of ocean; the latter 70,700 square miles.

Discipline broke down so completely in the new Marine Nationale, that in Toulon in September 1792 mutinous sailors hanged several naval officers from lampposts. (AC)

Convoying also reduced the opportunity for merchant ships to be taken once found. Normally merchant vessels risked attack by individual privateers (privately owned warships, licensed by a government), or national navy cruisers (typically a sloop-of-war or frigate, with 10 to 40 guns). Sometimes, privateers acted in pairs. A squadron of two to five cruisers might operate in concert.

An unescorted individual merchantman was almost certain to be captured by a lone cruiser that spotted it. The warship was typically faster, better armed and more heavily manned than a merchant vessel. If unescorted merchantmen sailing in company were discovered by a lone cruiser, typically only one would be taken. The merchant vessels would split up, and the cruiser could only chase after one at a time. Given enough time, the cruiser could find the other ships after taking the one it pursued. A stern chase is a long chase, and the unpursued ships had a lot of ocean to hide in.

With an escorted convoy, the raiding cruiser had to contend with an armed escort. The cruiser had to capture its prize and carry it away before the escort could interfere. A careless raider might find itself entangled with a would-be capture when the escort ships neared and became a prize instead of a prize-taker. Even a weak escort forced cruisers into hit-and-run tactics. Capturing one ship from a convoy was a good haul. A large convoy could expect to lose only a few ships, even when attacked.

Convoy dynamics worked – as long as the convoys were attacked by individual warships and privateers or by small squadrons of cruisers. They were vulnerable to attacks by fleets. A fleet of ships-of-the-line would rip through the escort. It also had enough vessels to attack multiple ships. Additionally, while privateers or commerce-raiding national warships were generally more interested in taking prizes than in destroying shipping, a fleet would often destroy the ships it could not provide prize crews for. This was one reason why Britain used convoys more often than France. Britain always had fleets at sea. France less so.

CANONNIER EN 1793

The Marine Royale had an excellent corps of naval gunners. The corps was suppressed by Saint André and the Committee on the grounds it resembled an aristocracy. As a result, the great guns were manned by untrained men, with gunnery accuracy suffering. (AC)

This also explains why the size and scope of the campaign grew with the government's concern for the safety of the convoy. Initially Van Stabel was sent with two ships-of-the-line, two frigates and a corvette. This was a respectable escort for a convoy, even one in excess of 100 ships.

A pair of ships-of-the-line with accompanying smaller ships was sufficient protection against individual cruisers or cruiser squadrons of two to four ships. Britain routinely assigned this size of escort to convoys sailing waters where privateers or cruisers were active. A determined group of cruisers might pick off individual merchantmen, but even the loss of a dozen ships would have been unimportant.

However, the Committee for Public Safety worried this escort would be insufficient. First, they assigned a squadron from Rochefort – five ships-of-the-line, two frigates, and a corvette – to join the escort. They then ordered the Brest Fleet – dubbed the Grand Fleet – to sail and cover the convoy.

Since the action of sending the Brest Fleet to sea had the effect of causing the Channel Fleet to enter the Atlantic in pursuit, an argument can be made that ordering the Brest Fleet out increased the chances of the convoy's interception. Yet given the importance placed on the convoy, it made sense to protect it as well as possible. Since the convoy's destination was Brest, it was an obvious target for the Royal Navy once it neared Ushant. In the age of sail, a convoy that size could easily spend a week from the time it reached the western approaches to Brittany until it entered the safety of the Goulet and the Inner Water.

Viilaret-Joyeuse seems to have realized the difficulty. His orders were to escort the convoy. Once the Channel Fleet made contact with his force, he ignored these orders. Rather, he followed a strategy of luring the Channel Fleet away from the convoy. This was probably the wisest course he could have followed.

Had he found the convoy, even if he placed his battle-line between the Channel Fleet and the convoy, merchant ship losses would have been heavy. The frigates and sloops attached to the Channel Fleet could have flanked the French battle line. Using superior British seamanship, they would have peeled off individual grain carriers while the French battle line was pinned by the Channel Fleet. Howe would have sent his light units off almost reflexively, hoping his opponent would detach ships-of-the-line from his battle line. This would allow Howe an advantage in the fleet battle that Howe desired.

Instead, Villaret-Joyeuse chose to draw the Channel Fleet away from the oncoming convoy, even adding ships from Nielly's Rochefort Squadron to keep the target attractive. Evidence that this was planned is shown by Villaret-Joyeuse's behaviour after it was clear the Channel Fleet was returning to port. The Brest Fleet also returned to port – before the convoy reached the French coast.

THE CAMPAIGN

OPENING MOVES, AUTUMN 1793 TO APRIL 1794

Harvest season in autumn 1793 opened with crop failure in France. The weather had been uncooperative that summer, but the political climate was worse. Revolution had been raging in France since 1789, but 1793 convulsed with counter-revolution. Open rebellion against the revolutionaries sprang up in Western France – Brittany, Maine-et-Loire, the Vendée and Loire-Atlantique – and in the south, near Toulon. France was fighting Austria and Prussia on their north-west frontier, Spain and the Italian States in the south, and Britain just about everywhere. The turmoil left too many French fields untilled. Even where a crop was sown, bad weather and fighting led to low yields.

The normal response to a food shortage was to import food. There were surpluses in Europe. Yet Revolutionary France had systematically alienated most of its neighbours. No one in Europe was willing to sell food to France. The nearest available source of food was the new United States. It had a crop surplus, felt grateful to France for assisting American independence, and viewed the French government as fellow republicans. The French ambassador to the United States, Edmond-Charles Genêt, paused his efforts to recruit privateers and raise armies of Americans to fight for France, to begin arranging purchases of grain and other food.

France's West Indian colonies were another source of food. Uprisings in Guadeloupe, Martinique and Saint Domingue (today's Haiti) and war with Britain interrupted trade with the home country in 1792 and 1793. The islands held sugar and other crops awaiting shipment. Many French ship owners were unwilling to sail directly to France from the Americas. Merchant ships were vulnerable to enemy warships – both privateers and naval cruisers – when sailing individually. They wanted an escort.

As 1793 wound to a close, plans were drawn to combine United States grain and West Indies produce together and ship everything to France in a single,

Edmond-Charles Genêt, Revolutionary France's ambassador to the United States, was responsible for purchasing grain in the United States and chartering ships for its transport to France. (AC)

The convoy assembled in Chesapeake Bay, anchoring off Hampton Roads. This allowed the merchant vessels to wait in neutral waters, unmolested by British cruisers. Cape Henry (shown) marked the entrance to the Chesapeake. (AC)

massive convoy. In the winter months of 1793 and 1794, French and American merchantmen began assembling in the Chesapeake, where they could wait until an escort was assembled.

Chesapeake Bay was the perfect assembly point. A large, sheltered estuary within United States territorial waters where French ships could wait, anchored in Hampton Roads, unmolested by British warships. The Chesapeake was centrally located, virtually equidistant from Georgia and Massachusetts, making it a convenient assembly point. Food could move along the American Atlantic coast to the Chesapeake in US ships, cargoes shipped from one domestic port to another. It would take a bold British cruiser to seize the ships, even if its captain was certain the food was ultimately headed to France. No Admiralty court would view such a ship as a lawful prize.

The convoy was to be large. Initially it was hoped it might total 350 ships, a massive assembly of shipping in the 18th century. It would not sail until spring. In the winter, the North Atlantic is lashed by storms which would scatter a convoy, possibly sinking many ships. Mariners feared the perils of the sea far more than the hazards of combat and the winter North Atlantic has more than its share of those perils. Meanwhile, the ships could gather in safety.

As 1793 ended, the French sent an escort for the convoy from Brest. On 26 December (or 6 Nivôse Year II in the France's Revolutionary calendar) a squadron of two ships-of-the line, two frigates and a brig-corvette set sail from Brest. Under the command of Contre-Amiral Van Stabel it set out for North America, reaching the Chesapeake on 12 February.

While Van Stabel's squadron was crossing the Atlantic, changes were coming to the Marine National. In January the Constituent Assembly adopted a new flag, the familiar French Tricolour on a white field. It replaced the white and gold Royal fleur-de-lis flag. It would fly over French warships thereafter.

The period known as 'The Reign of Terror' was reaching its peak in the winter of 1793–94. The anti-revolutionary, pro-Royalist uprisings in rural France as well as the surrender of Toulon to France's enemies by Royalists were answered by judicial violence by the Revolutionary government. Traitors were found everywhere, and executed as quickly as they were denounced. In the winter of 1794, the Constituent Assembly concluded that the Marine Nationale lacked sufficient revolutionary zeal, as evidenced by the turmoil at Brest and Toulon.

To encourage the navy's performance, the Constituent Assembly issued a decree regulating the behaviour of French ships in battle. It stated no ship-of-the-line could surrender, regardless of the odds against it, unless and until it was so damaged that it was sinking. Frigates and corvettes could not surrender unless facing odds of at least two to one against them and then only if so damaged as to be sinking. Should a ship surrender before those conditions were met, its officers would be pronounced traitors to their country and executed. It was an insult to the Marine Nationale, and unlikely to improve the performance of a warship in battle.

Ambassador Genêt complicated French planning. Sometime during the winter, he sent dispatches to France. The correspondence indicated he planned to split the convoy, sending part of it early with a light escort – perhaps only frigates. Or possibly Genêt was unclear. Since the convoy actually departed in one body, he may have been complaining Van Stabel's escort was too light. Regardless, he triggered a reaction from the French Marine Ministry. Fearing part of the convoy had sailed without an escort, it sent a second squadron to protect them.

On 10 April, Contre-Amiral Nielly sailed from Rochefort with five ships-of-the-line and several frigates and corvettes. Other frigates and corvettes had left Rochefort earlier with instructions to find the unsent advance convoy and direct that convoy's commander to rendezvous with Nielly 100 leagues west of Belle-Isle (roughly 47 deg., 22 min North, 9 deg. West).

The next day, 11 April, on the other side of the Atlantic and unknown to Nielly and the Maritime Ministry, the convoy finally raised anchor and

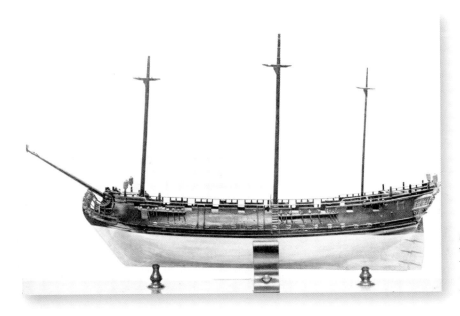

Many of the vessels carrying food cargoes looked similar to this ship-rigged merchantman. Most could carry between 100 and 300 tons of cargo. (AC)

HOW IMPORTANT WAS THE GRAIN CONVOY?

One of the most oft-repeated elements of this campaign was the critical need for the safe arrival of the grain convoy. Without it, historians assert, the Revolutionary Government would have collapsed due to the subsequent famine. But was that true? Could any single convoy carry enough food to make a difference?

The convoy was large. Most British sources state it contained between 107 and 117 merchant vessels. French sources state it was 170 ships. The size of individual ships in the convoy is unknown, but an average cargo capacity of 300 tons would be a safe estimate. Some of the convoy would consist of West Indiamen. These ranged in size from 300 tons to 750 tons. Other ships would have made up the balance and some of these would be smaller: 50 to 250 tons.

The food carried would have been dried and much of it would have been grain: rice from French colonies or Georgia; wheat,

Guadeloupe (shown) was one of France's two West Indies sugar islands. West Indiamen, typically of between 300 and 600 tons displacement, carried the sugar to France, but the war forced them to await convoy in the Chesapeake. (AC)

barley and maize from the United States. Some might have been preserved fish and meat. A percentage would have been sugar from Guadeloupe and Martinique. One pound of the convoyed food would have fed one person for one day, perhaps not to satisfaction, but enough for survival. One ton would have fed roughly 75 people for one month; a 300-ton vessel would have carried enough food to feed 22,500 for one month.

Given low British estimates of 107 ships, this would have been enough food to feed 600,000 people for four months (a period long enough to bring in the harvest for 1794). If the French total of 170 ships was correct, the convoy would have fed over 950,000 people for four months.

In 1794 France's population was between 27 and 28 million. The convoy would not feed all of France, but there was no need to do that. There was food in France despite the 1793 crop failure, just not enough. In eastern and southern France a river and canal system ensured surplus food could move to areas of shortage.

In western France, particularly Brittany, and the western maritime coast of the Atlantic, there were no convenient waterways. Food had to travel by wagon. That meant imports had to arrive by sea. And this was the area most affected by crop failure. In 1794 the population of Brittany (the province containing Brest) was around 700,000. The convoy's food would bridge an important part of the shortfall in this area.

It definitely would ensure the population loyal to the revolutionary government in that region was well fed. Since Brittany and the Atlantic maritime was the heart of anti-revolutionary activity, securing Brest, Lorient and Rochefort went a long way to ensuring the defeat of the Vendée counter-revolution. Had Howe stopped the convoy, or even taken a big fraction of it, Republican France could have lost these bases, and the Vendée uprising succeeded.

Yet even if the convoy failed to arrive, the revolutionaries might have succeeded in holding these bases. The counter-revolutionaries were a group that never missed an opportunity to miss an opportunity. They could have easily botched the chance of destruction of the grain convoy offered.

departed the Chesapeake. No exact tally of the total number of vessels was recorded and estimates of the total number of ships in the convoy vary. The only agreement was that it was much less than the 350 originally rumoured. Some British and American historians claim it contained 117 vessels; others 130. Most French historians list the total as 170 merchantmen. Regardless, it was a massive assembly of ships. It probably covered a patch of ocean ten miles square once it was at sea. While the core of the convoy would have covered a three-square mile area straggling, running (surging ahead of the convoy) and a merchant captain's dislike of sailing too closely to other vessels would have ensured a wide footprint.

Word of the convoy, along with attendant rumours, washed along both sides of the Atlantic. The French knew of it. The British knew of it. The world knew of it. Howe kept his fleet safely in port during the winter months, but he expected to intercept the convoy when the time came. That would probably be in May. Assuming the French waited until after the winter storms and

Rochefort was France's second-largest Atlantic naval port in 1794. Nielly's squadron sailed from this port. (AC)

the equinoctial gales were past, the convoy would sail in April. Crossing the Atlantic with a convoy of ill-matched vessels would take at least six weeks.

Besides, Howe had his own series of convoys to worry over. The annual East Indies convoy was scheduled to sail at the end of April. It was as tempting a prize to the French as the rumoured grain convoy was to the British – in some ways more so. While the French convoy carried mainly food (including valuable sugar), the cargoes of the East Indies convoy included iron goods, tin, woollens and manufactured goods – all of value to France's wartime needs. There were also routine convoys inbound and outbound from Newfoundland and the West Indies, as well as convoys carrying goods to and from Ireland that were in the Atlantic. With at least one set of French ships-of-the-line abroad in the Atlantic (Van Stabel's squadron) and more threatening to take to sea, Howe was holding outbound ships in Britain, collecting them at Portsmouth and anchoring them at St Helens, a roadstead off the Isle of Wight.

Howe regularly had frigates monitoring Brest during the late winter and early autumn months. From February to the end of April they reported Villaret-Joyeuse's fleet still snug in its harbour. Finally, 2 May 1794 he took the Channel Fleet to sea, escorting 99 merchant ships of the East India convoy.

CONVOY ACTIONS, 2–16 MAY

It took Howe two days to sail down the Channel from Spithead and St Helens. By 4 May he was off the Lizard, a peninsula on the south-east coast of Cornwall and the most southerly point of Britain. This marked the entrance to the Atlantic Ocean. At this point the East India convoy broke away from the Channel Fleet.

It had an escort of two ships-of-the-line, two two-decker warships, a frigate and a sloop. These would accompany the convoy to its destination. Additionally, East Indiamen were heavily armed for merchant ships, equivalent in firepower, if not fighting ability, to small frigates. But Howe

CAPTURE OF THE *CASTOR* BY THE *SANS PAREIL* (PP. 40–41)

A frigate stands little chance against a ship-of-the-line. It stands even less chance when the frigate is a 32-gun ship with 12-pdrs on its gun deck, and its opponent is one big French two-deck 80-gun second-rate ship-of-the-line with 36-pdrs on its lower deck, 24-pdrs on its upper deck, and 12-pdrs on the quarterdeck and forecastle. When a ship's heaviest guns are equal to the opponent's lightest guns, there is no shame in running. Even if you are the only warship guarding a convoy of over 30 merchant ships carrying dried fish from Newfoundland to Britain – if you run into a ship-of-the-line, you should run.

That was the situation Thomas Troubridge, then captain of the 32-gun *Castor* (**1**), found he faced on 9 May 1794. Actually, it was worse than that. Not only was he facing the 80-gun *Sans Pareil* (**2**), but that ship was accompanied by four French 74s and a half-dozen frigates and corvettes (**3**). Troubridge stood towards them to investigate their identity. Once he discovered what he was up against, all he could do was signal the convoy to scatter (**4**). And have run *Castor*, too.

Today many believe a frigate could always outrun a ship-of-the-line. In reality, it depends on the sea state, the wind and the two ships. *Castor* was an Amazon-class frigate; good ships, but not known for an outstanding turn of speed. *Sans Pareil* was a Témeraire-class ship-of-the-line, famed as speedy ships. *Castor* would have lost momentum and running room in turning away from *Sans Pareil*. *Sans Pareil* was moving at a full clip towards *Castor*. Plus the French frigates and corvettes would have served as beaters in a hunt, hemming *Castor*'s movements.

The chase would be a short one. A fight would have been hopeless. When *Sans Pareil* came within range, its captain would have fired one shot ahead of *Castor*, a signal for the ship to stop. *Castor*, in response, would have backed its topsails, lowered its colours, and lain hove-to, motionless, awaiting a prize crew.

was aware that French squadrons, including some containing ships-of-the-line, were at sea and that the Brest Fleet had the potential to sail. He therefore detached six 74-gun ships-of-the-line and two frigates under the command of Rear Admiral George Montagu to accompany the convoy as far south as the longitude of Cape Finisterre.

Once south of Finisterre, the French fleet would pose no further danger to the convoy. Howe gave Montagu orders to break off from the convoy at that latitude and search for the French grain convoy. Montagu parted company from the convoy on 11 May, and conducted the patrol assigned by Howe, cruising north–south between Cape Ortegal and the latitude of Belle Isle. This was a line that covered most of the Bay of Biscay, but stopped south of the approaches to Brest.

Detaching Montagu's squadron left the Channel Fleet with 26 ships-of-the-line. Howe took this force to Ushant, reaching it on 5 May. He sent two frigates, backed by a ship-of-the-line to reconnoitre Brest. They reported seeing a ship-of-the-line, two frigates and a corvette anchored in Camaret Bay, with 22 other ships, which they presumed were ships-of-the-line in the Goulet. Howe assumed the French fleet would sail to support the convoy. This would provide an opportunity to fight and defeat the French. Not wanting to discourage the French fleet from departing Brest, he sailed into the Atlantic, steering south-west. He searched for the convoy, sailing south-west for a week without result, before turning around on 12 May.

Howe had missed Nielly's squadron by nearly a month. By the time Howe set up his search in the Atlantic, Nielly was north and west of Howe, off Ireland. Two of Nielly's questing scouts, the frigate *Atalante* and corvette *Levrette*, found a convoy outbound from Cork on 5 May. When they investigated, they discovered the escort included two ships-of-the-line, 74-gun *Swiftsure* and 64-gun *St Albans*. The two British warships took off in pursuit of the French cruisers, which split up and ran. *Levrette* managed to outpace *St Albans*, but *Swiftsure* lived up to its name and ran down *Atalante* after a two-day chase.

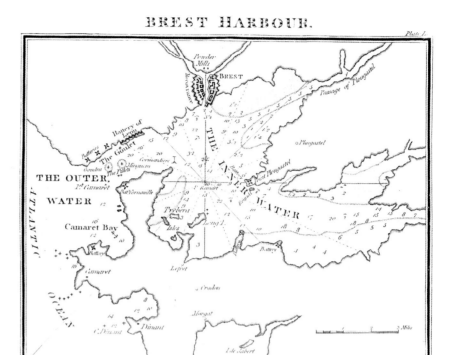

Atalante's captain, Charles Linois, put up a stout defence, but surrendered to *Swiftsure* after taking heavy casualties. *Swiftsure* had no sooner transferred a prize crew to *Atalante* when three French ships-of-the-line from Nielly's squadron were spotted. Captor and prize fled the new arrivals, escaping at sunset. Both arrived safely at Cork a few days later.

Two days later it was Nielly's turn. On 9 May, off Cape Clear, Nielly stumbled on a homeward-bound British convoy from Newfoundland. Its sole escort was the 32-gun frigate *Castor*, skippered by Captain Thomas Troubridge. The convoy's 30 ships scattered, pursued by French warships. Nielly's flagship, the 80-gun *Sans Pareil* challenged *Castor*, quickly capturing the frigate. Taking most of the British crew, including Troubridge, aboard *Sans Pareil*, Nielly left only 20 British sailors on *Castor*. He also held a drumhead prize court, condemning *Castor* as a lawful prize. Nielly commissioned it as a frigate in the Marine Nationale, manning it with officers and men from his squadron.

Most of the convoy's merchantmen were captured. Some prizes, ten ships filled with salt fish from Newfoundland, were sent to France escorted by the 20-gun *Maire-Guiton*. The prize convoy ran into Montagu's squadron on 15 May. The British retook the ten sail and the corvette. It was the first positive evidence anyone in the Channel Fleet had that French ships-of-the-line (other than Van Stabel's two) were loose in the Atlantic. Montagu detached a frigate to find and inform Howe that the French were out.

The dispatches also requested reinforcements. If Nielly combined with Van Stabel, the convoy would have seven ships-of-the-line to Montagu's six. Moreover, the French would have at least six frigates and corvettes. Montagu, having detached one of his two, had one remaining frigate. Despite the odds,

Montagu turned his squadron west, hoping to find the convoy before the two French squadrons could combine.

Meanwhile the grain convoy kept plodding east – more slowly than Van Stabel would likely have desired. It was only averaging a little over 2 knots, perhaps 2.5 knots on a good day, between 50 and 60 nautical miles travelled each day. There were many reasons for this slow speed, but the most important one was that a convoy had to travel at a speed lower than the best speed of its slowest ship. Otherwise that ship could not catch up if it fell behind. Throw in a bunch of individualistic merchant masters unused to sailing in formation and more comfortable sailing alone, and you had a recipe for disorder, which slowed the convoy even more.

Unknown to Van Stabel, the convoy's slow speed worked to its advantage. There were two large British formations in the eastern Atlantic, one near the rendezvous point Nielly had set. Meanwhile, Nielly was nowhere near the rendezvous. He was off the Irish coast, trying to draw the British north by revealing his ships there.

The Ministry in Paris continued worrying over the fate of the convoy. The progress of the Channel Fleet and its attendant convoy down the Channel had been observed in both Britain and France. (It was hard to conceal a force of that size in those narrow waters.) This inflamed concern in Paris about the convoy's fate. Something more had to be done to guarantee its safety. Orders were sent to Villaret-Joyeuse to take the Brest Fleet to sea in order to protect the convoy.

To ensure Villaret-Joyeuse faithfully executed his orders, the Committee had Saint-André accompany the fleet. Issued plenipotentiary powers to run the fleet and remove and even execute officers, Saint-André sailed aboard Villaret-Joyeuse's flagship, the three-deck, 120-gun *Montagne*. Laid down in 1786 as *États de Bourgogne*, and completed in 1791, it had been renamed *Côte d'Or* when war with Britain started in 1793, and finally *Montagne* (after the dominant party in the Assembly) in September 1793. It was the lead ship of four three-deckers ordered immediately after the end of the Wars of American Independence.

The Brest Fleet, styled The Grand Fleet of France, weighed anchor at 5:30pm on 16 May. It sailed out of The Goulet into the Outer Water and into the Atlantic Ocean. The way was temporarily clear. On 16 May Howe was four days out from his turn-around point and three days from reaching the entrance to Brest. Villaret-Joyeuse, with 25 ships-of-the-line (including four three-deckers) and 15 or 16 frigates and corvettes sailed into the freedom of the ocean. As night fell the fleet was blanketed by a thick evening fog.

ESCAPE AND PURSUIT OF THE FRENCH FLEET

It turned out the two fleets, the Channel Fleet and the Grand Fleet of France, passed each other during the night of 17 May, possibly coming within hailing distance of each other. The north-east wind which assisted the departure of the French Fleet from Brest also triggered a thick fog that persisted until daybreak on 18 May. The fog covering the Atlantic shrouded the two opponents from each other. French lookouts reported hearing bells and beating drums used by the British as fog signals. Yet both sides stuck to the courses charted by their

Slipping Past the Channel Fleet in the Fog

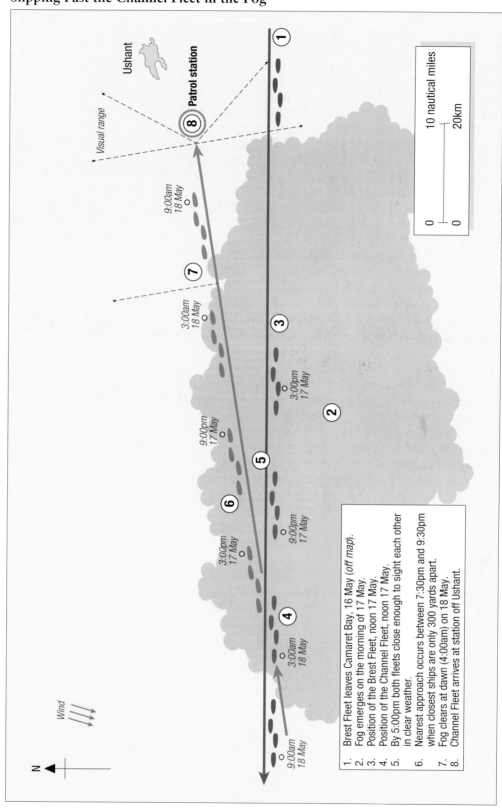

Ushant

Visual range

Patrol station

Wind

N

9:00am
18 May

3:00am
18 May

9:00pm
17 May

3:00pm
17 May

9:00am
18 May

3:00am
18 May

9:00pm
17 May

3:00pm
17 May

3:00pm
17 May

9:00pm
17 May

3:00am
18 May

9:00am
18 May

1. Brest Fleet leaves Camaret Bay, 16 May (*off map*).
2. Fog emerges on the morning of 17 May.
3. Position of the Brest Fleet, noon 17 May.
4. Position of the Channel Fleet, noon 17 May.
5. By 5:00pm both fleets close enough to sight each other in clear weather.
6. Nearest approach occurs between 7:30pm and 9:30pm when closest ships are only 300 yards apart.
7. Fog clears at dawn (4:00am) on 18 May.
8. Channel Fleet arrives at station off Ushant.

0 — 10 nautical miles
0 — 20km

respective commanders, with the French heading just a little north of west, while the British followed an east-north-east track to Ushant. When the skies cleared on the following day, the seas around both fleets were empty of enemy ships.

What could have happened if the fog lifted while the two fleets were in sight of each other is one of history's great 'what ifs'. The French would have almost certainly lost any general engagement, at least in any meaningful sense. The British outnumbered the French 26 ships-of-the-line to 25. By 1 June those numbers had flipped thanks to battle casualties and French reinforcements. Yet even with improved odds France still lost seven ships-of-the-line. That the French would have done better with worse odds and without ten days in which to shake down the ships unmolested by the British is hard to credit.

At best, the French could have fought an inconclusive battle and slipped back to Brest or further out into the Atlantic. Returning to Brest would have defeated the purpose of protecting the grain convoy (and likely cost Villaret-Joyeuse his head). Sailing further out into the Atlantic would have postponed the battle a day, as actually occurred on 28 and 29 May. Howe would have pursued and continued the action on the following days. Ultimately a battle with an outcome similar to that seen on 1 June would have occurred within the week.

Thomas Troubridge would gain fame commanding a ship-of-the-line at the battles of St Vincent and the Nile. He was also present at the First of June, but as a French prisoner aboard *Sans Pareil*, after his frigate was captured by Nielly's squadron. (AC)

Either result would have resulted in the British being between the convoy and Brest. Howe would have been closer to the Channel ports. He could have got his prizes and damaged ships to Plymouth more quickly. He would have been in a better position to get his fleet back out to sea, and likely would have been off Brest when the grain convoy reached French waters. Although the convoy might have diverted to Lorient or Bordeaux, it would almost certainly have taken losses with the Channel Fleet in the offing.

Or possibly, Howe would have taken his prizes to Portsmouth, celebrated his victory and let the grain convoy reach Brest unmolested. Regardless, when the fog cleared each of the two fleets was unaware of the other fleet's presence. Villaret-Joyeuse continued westward, seeking the grain convoy or Nielly's squadron. Howe continued to Ushant.

On 19 May, the day after Howe arrived off Ushant, he sent two frigates, *Phaeton* and *Latona*, backed by the *Caesar* (80), and *Leviathan* (74) to examine Brest. They returned at 8:00pm, reporting that the harbour was empty. *Leviathan*'s captain spoke to the captain of a United States ship in the area who reported the French had sailed a few days back. That evening, he was met by the frigate sent by Montagu, which reported the capture of the *Maire-Guiton*, as well as Nielly's attack on the Newfoundland convoy and Nielly's intention to rendezvous with the escort of the grain convoy.

Howe's Pursuit of the French Fleet

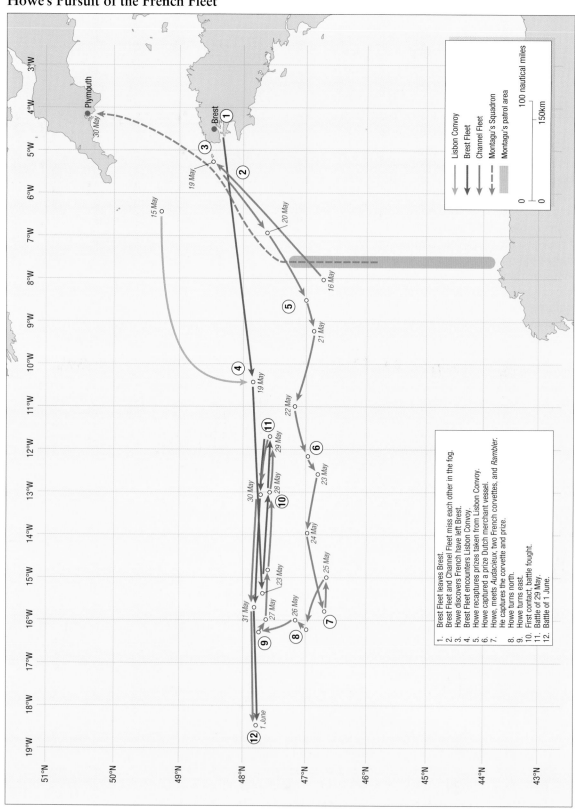

1. Brest Fleet leaves Brest.
2. Brest Fleet and Channel Fleet miss each other in the fog.
3. Howe discovers French have left Brest.
4. Brest Fleet encounters Lisbon Convoy.
5. Howe recaptures prizes taken from Lisbon Convoy.
6. Howe captured a prize Dutch merchant vessel.
7. Howe, meets *Audacieux*, two French corvettes, and *Rambler*. He captures the corvette and prize.
8. Howe turns north.
9. Howe turns east.
10. First contact, battle fought.
11. Battle of 29 May.
12. Battle of 1 June.

Lisbon Convoy
Brest Fleet
Channel Fleet
Montagu's Squadron
Montagu's patrol area

100 nautical miles

150km

In 1794 *Montagne* was France's most modern and powerful three-deck ship-of-the-line. It had been launched as *États de Bourgogne*, renamed *Côte d'Or* when the Republic was established, and renamed yet again for the party holding power in 1794 (The Mountain). It was renamed *Ocean* in 1795 and served the French navies under that name for a further 50 years. (AC)

The frigate also reported Montagu planned to sail his squadron north and south along the seven degrees west longitude between 47 degrees north and 43 degrees 30 minutes north. Howe feared seven degrees west 48 degrees north was the destination of Joyeuse-Villaret's fleet. Montagu's six 74s would be easy prey for the Brest Fleet. At 4:00am on 20 May, about an hour before dawn he ordered the Channel Fleet west, in pursuit of the French and relief of Montagu.

The French spent 19 May sailing west. Their course took them through a Dutch convoy heading for Lisbon: 53 merchant ships escorted by the Dutch frigate *Alliance* and corvette *Waalzaamheid*. The United Provinces were then at war with Republican France and the Grand Fleet tore into the convoy, scattering it. The Dutch escorts were less inclined to last-ditch defence than the Royal Navy. *Castor* and fled, making successful escapes. The French took 18 to 20 prizes before the rest of the merchantmen evaded their pursuers.

The Grand Fleet was also joined by *Patroite*, a 74 from Nielly's squadron, with a report on Nielly's actions. This raised the French line-of-battle to 26 ships.

Howe charted a course west-southwest through noon on 21 May. He sailed through the supposed rendezvous point for Nielly's squadron and the grain convoy shortly after noon on 20 May. It was empty: no convoy, no enemy squadron and no sight of Montagu. At 2:00am on 21 May, lookouts reported a strange fleet. It proved to be 16 prizes captured from the Lisbon convoy, sailing for France. Over the next two hours ten of the vessels were recaptured. Howe, not wishing to reduce his crews prior to an impending battle, decided against keeping the prizes and, having removed their crews, burnt them.

Interrogating the prisoners, the British learned the French had been 120 to 180 miles from them (at 47 degrees, 46 minutes north, 11 degrees, 22 minutes west) earlier that day. They also learned the French fleet had grown to 26 ships-of-the-line but was down to four frigates. (The rest were escorting prizes, carrying messages to and from Nielly or Van Stabel, or out

The Channel Fleet left Spithead on 2 May. By then Nielly's squadron had already been at sea for three weeks, having left Rochefort on 10 April. (AC)

scouting.) Questioning revealed Saint-André was aboard *Montagne*, and the French wanted a close-quarter fight. That was something the Royal Navy wanted too.

Since the French ships were now known to be west and north of both Howe and Montagu, and Montagu was south and east of Howe, Howe decided Montagu was safe. The Channel Fleet was between the French and Montagu and would have to go through Howe to reach Montagu's squadron. At noon on 21 May, Howe shifted his course almost due west, in pursuit of the French fleet, seeking to close with it.

Villaret-Joyeuse was also taking his ships due west, on a line halfway between the 47th and 48th parallels. He was moving more slowly than Howe, barely walking speed, averaging a little more than 60 nautical miles per day. He was 30 to 40 miles north of the track Howe was following. Being further west Villaret-Joyeuse still had a considerable lead on Howe, but Howe was closing.

Meanwhile, Villaret-Joyeuse was waiting for the grain convoy. Once it reached a longitude of 15 degrees west his fleet would protect it. In the meantime he did not yet want to chain his fleet to the convoy. He felt he needed freedom to manoeuvre, and interpose his fleet between the British and the convoy. He was keeping tabs on the convoy with his frigates and corvettes, shuttling them between the convoy and his fleet.

When his fleet left Brest, he had 16 of these scouts. Nielly had at least as many frigates and corvettes as ships-of-the-line when he left Rochefort. Yet Villaret-Joyeuse only kept four with his fleet. By this point Nielly likely only had two. Historians remain unsure of the exact number of French frigates and corvettes that participated in the campaign. Even the names of most are unknown. Republican France kept poor and incomplete records.

Howe felt that Villaret-Joyeuse was close. At 8:00am on 23 May, his fleet found three more Dutch merchant ships captured by the French from the Lisbon convoy. They had parted from the French fleet two days earlier. The British had been sailing west south-west since noon on 22 May. When the wind shifted at noon on 23 May, they changed to a course slightly north of west, before doglegging back to west-south-west at noon on 24 May. Unknown to Howe, the Grand Fleet was less than 60 miles north-west of the Channel Fleet when Howe ordered the change. Villaret-Joyeuse had doubled back, heading due east from noon on 23 May. This course change would take the British away from the French.

The next morning, prior to sunrise, but when twilight made ships visible, the Channel Fleet sighted four sails. The ships proved to be *Audacieux* (74), towing a merchant brig, and the corvettes *Républicaine* and *Inconnue*. These ships had departed Nielly's squadron the previous night and were seeking the Grand Fleet. The British *Audacious* (also a 74) and frigate *Niger* gave chase, followed by the lead elements of the Channel Fleet. *Audacieux* slipped its tow and made its escape. The other three ships were snapped up by the British. Howe burned the three captured

ships, again refusing to weaken his crews before a major battle by sending off prize crews.

The merchant brig proved to be an American brig, *Rambler*. The unfortunate brig had been caught by the French while carrying a cargo of wine from Falmouth to Philadelphia. Since France was at war with Britain, despite being a neutral ship sailing to a neutral destination its port of departure made *Rambler* a legitimate prize for the French.

To communicate between the convoy, Nielly's squadron, and the Brest Fleet, the French made extensive use of frigates, deploying them as scouts and couriers throughout the campaign. (AC)

The American brig *Rambler* probably resembled the ship pictured, the 139-ton *Alert* from Newburyport, Massachusetts. Although *Rambler* was a neutral it was a lawful prize, because the French caught it carrying a cargo from Britain. (AC)

Howe knew the French fleet was somewhere nearby. Each set of prisoners reported its position at the time their ship had separated from the Grand Fleet, or the rendezvous point for the fleet to which the ship was heading. In all cases it was close. The problem was that a ship more than 15 miles away was over the horizon, and invisible. Even spacing his frigates in a line at signalling distance (around five miles during daytime) only a small part of the ocean would be swept. All Howe could do was keep sweeping until he got lucky and spotted the French.

Howe had sailed 100 miles past the French rendezvous without finding Villaret-Joyeuse. At this point Howe sailed north-west, casting about for Villaret-Joyeuse, then at 6:00am on 26 May, tacked east. At noon he again turned, north, sailing 30 miles before realizing the French had left that patch of ocean. Realizing they must have become east of him, he ordered the Channel Fleet on a course almost due east. He rushed east, covering over 120 nautical miles over the next 24 hours. At 6:30am on 28 May, British lookout frigates reported a strange fleet to the east. It was the Grand Fleet.

BATTLE OF 28 MAY

The day of 28 May dawned with the wind from the south by west, or 11.25 degrees west of due south. The wind was brisk, perhaps 22 to 27 knots, with a choppy sea and a lot of spray. When the British lookouts spotted the French the Grand Fleet was directly to windward, upwind of the Channel Fleet. That gave the French the weather gauge. (The downwind fleet was said to hold the lee gauge.) That meant to engage the British had to claw into the wind, a slow process.

That assumed it was the French fleet. At 6:30am all that could be made out were masts and a few sails. At ten miles, the ships were hull-down, below the horizon, hidden by the curvature of the Earth. It could easily have been another batch of Dutch or British merchantmen captured by the French rather than the French battle fleet at that point. It could even have been the grain fleet. (At the time, the grain fleet was within sight of the Grand Fleet, although the British did not know this.)

At 8:15am Howe ordered a squadron of four 74s to investigate the strange sails. These were *Bellerophon*, *Russell*, *Marlborough* and *Thunderer*. Howe's four fastest ships-of-the-line, they had been formed into a flying squadron led by the junior admiral present, Rear Admiral Sir Thomas Pasley aboard *Bellerophon*. By 9:00am, these ships confirmed Howe's hopes. The British had found the French Fleet. Howe ordered his fleet to clear for action. He ordered the flying squadron to shorten sail, to allow the fleet to catch up to them.

Howe also recalled the frigates, which were scouting, and ordered them to take their assigned stations during a fleet action. Initially this placed the frigates between the flying squadron and the main fleet. Once a formal line-of-battle exchange began, the frigates would distribute themselves on the disengaged

1.	Howe releases the flying squadron to investigate the French.	**5.**	*Bellerophon* falls away from *Révolutionaire*.
2.	*Révolutionaire* begins falling behind to engage the British ships.	**6.**	Multiple ships of the Flying Squadron and lead ships in the original line of battle engage *Révolutionaire*.
3.	Howe orders a general chase.		
4.	*Bellerophon* engages *Révolutionaire* and fights by itself for over an hour.	**7.**	Howe orders fleet to form line of battle around the flagship.

The Battle of 28 May

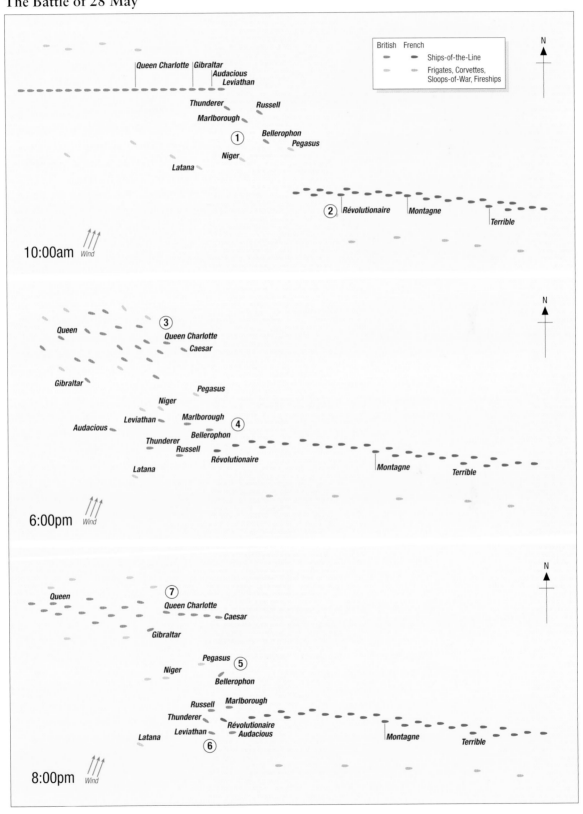

British   French
● ● Ships-of-the-Line
● ● Frigates, Corvettes,
Sloops-of-War, Fireships

N

Queen Charlotte | Gibraltar
Audacious
Leviathan

Thunderer   Russell
Marlborough
① Bellerophon
Pegasus
Niger
Latana

② Révolutionaire   Montagne
Terrible

10:00am *Wind*

N

Queen   ③
Queen Charlotte
Caesar

Gibraltar

Pegasus
Niger
Leviathan   Marlborough
Audacious   ④ Bellerophon
Thunderer
Russell
Latana   Révolutionaire   Montagne   Terrible

6:00pm *Wind*

N

Queen   ⑦
Queen Charlotte
Caesar
Gibraltar

Pegasus   ⑤
Niger
Bellerophon

Russell   Marlborough
Thunderer
Révolutionaire
Latana   Leviathan   Audacious
⑥   Montagne   Terrible

8:00pm *Wind*

Rear Admiral Thomas Pasley was *Bellerophon*'s captain when the war started. After being promoted to rear admiral, Pasley remained aboard *Bellerophon*, using it as his flagship when Howe made Pasley head of the Flying Squadron. Pasley saw action on all three days of battle, losing a leg on 1 June. (AC)

side of the line-of-battle. Signal flags and fired guns were the only way for an admiral to send orders to other ships in a fleet during the days before radio communication. Gun commands were drowned out by combat gunfire once the action started, while the ships in the line of battle furthest from the flagship had their view of the flagship blocked by other ships in line. So, during the battle the frigates' job was to repeat the signals flown from the flagship, allowing blocked ships to receive the admiral's signals.

As the day opened on the French side of the battlefield they knew as much about the strange sails to the north of them as the British knew of the sails they spotted south of them. Initially they stood towards the Channel Fleet. When they were close enough to learn that they had not found another enemy convoy, they hauled up. Villaret-Joyeuse's orders allowed him to engage in a battle only if the French held the weather gauge, and only if necessary to protect the convoy.

While his fleet was upwind, Villaret-Joyeuse was not yet ready to concede a battle was necessary to protect the convoy. He had the wind, and was between the British and the convoy. Battles were risky things. If the French fleet were lost that day, the odds the British would find and destroy the convoy increased. Villaret-Joyeuse would prepare for battle, but not initiate it. Better to let the British force action than to sail down to meet the British. In order to reach the Grand Fleet, the Channel Fleet had to sail upwind, a slow process, which also kept the guns that could engage the French during the approach to a minimum. Villaret-Joyeuse's decision was approved by Saint André.

Howe had the 26 ships-of-the-line he departed Portsmouth with after detaching the convoy escort and Montagu's squadron. Villaret-Joyeuse had 27 – those which had sailed from Brest with him plus *Audacieux* and *Patriote* from Nielly's squadron, which joined Villaret-Joyeuse over the last two days.

Both sides cleared for action. This involved taking down all of the temporary partitions and furniture on the gun decks, quarterdeck and poop, and sending these into the hold, below the waterline. This left the upper decks clear of any objects that could be hit and splintered by gunfire. If possible livestock, pets and non-combatants were also sent below.

The cockpit, below the waterline and normally where the midshipmen (apprentice officers) berthed would be converted into a surgery. The midshipmen's sea chests were pushed together as an operating table. The surgeon and his mates cleaned and laid out the instruments.

The decks were watered down and strewn with sand. (The former dampened stray gunpowder spilled on the deck, reducing fire hazard; the latter improved traction on a deck slippery with water.) Chain slings were set on the spars to reduce the chance they would strike the deck if the rigging was shot away.

Galley fires – indeed all fires, except the slow match used to fire the guns – were doused. Good captains made sure their men went into battle well fed and in good spirits. If time permitted, as it did on this day, a final hot meal was cooked before dousing the fires and served to the crew. The day's spirit ration (typically rum for the British, brandy for the French) was issued as well. (At 11:10am Howe had signalled to send the hands to dinner.)

The great guns were released from the lashings used to secure them when sailing. The tools to operate them were distributed. Tubs were placed between every other pair of guns and filled with seawater used to swab out the guns prior to reloading. The guns would be manned, loaded and run out. Small arms – cutlasses, pikes and pistols – would be broken out and distributed to sailors detailed as boarders.

The difference between the two fleets was clear during these preparations and as the fleets arrayed for battle. The Channel Fleet, schooled by long practice, was ready for battle within an hour. Howe had his ships in two lines on the larboard (or port) tack (with the wind coming from the port side) with the flying squad ahead of the fleet, well to windward, and the frigates still between the flying squadron and the two lines of ships-of-the-line.

The French took much longer to prepare. Their crews rarely went to sea. Since many of their captains had been naval lieutenants or ensigns or from the merchant service the previous June, many were unfamiliar with signalling and unused to commanding a ship sailing in a close formation.

The French fleet lay to nine miles from the British. As Villaret-Joyeuse attempted to form a line of battle, disorder ruled. Captains of three ships of the line decided this was the time to change a topsail, one replaced the topsail yard. Other captains were slow to take their station. Finally the British observed a three-decker passing along the French line, passing close to each ship in turn. It was *Montagne*. A frustrated Villaret-Joyeuse had despaired of signalling orders, and going from ship to ship verbally giving orders about

Before a ship could fight it had to be cleared for action. All partitions and furniture on the gun decks would be placed in the hold, the guns unlashed and readied for combat, and the decks washed down with water and sanded. (AC)

Howe created a new system of signals and then put them in a small book he could carry in a pocket. This is a page from the signal book. (AC)

where they were supposed to be and what they were supposed to be doing. Finally the French formed into a ragged formation and made sail.

By then it was 1:00pm. Howe soon reacted to what he perceived as the French making off. At 1:30pm he ordered the flying squadron to harass the enemy's rear. Fifteen minutes later he signalled a general chase. This permitted the ships to leave the line of battle and make for the enemy at best speed. This was followed by a signal to 'engage the enemy as arriving up by him' or attack the enemy ship closest to you. He had not only slipped the leash, he had loosed the seadogs on the French.

Sailing-era naval battles were fought at walking speeds. It was 2:30pm before *Russell* drew close enough to the rearmost French ships to open fire. The French returned fire, with little to no damage done on either side. Although astern of the French line, *Russell* was finally upwind of the French. By 3:00pm *Bellerophon*, Pasley's flagship, had drawn abreast of the trailing French warship. *Bellerophon* tacked to starboard to close.

At 5:00pm the French van and centre shortened sail. They did so because the three-decker *Révolutionaire* was falling behind and Villaret-Joyeuse felt it needed to be supported. To the British it appeared the French were slowing so *Révolutionaire* could swap places with the trailing 74, the target of fire from *Bellerophon* and *Russell*. Yet *Révolutionaire*'s behaviour was contrary to Villaret-Joyeuse's and Saint André's intention to avoid a fight that day. *Révolutionaire*'s captain, M. Vaudangel, had fallen out of line, deliberately dawdling. Filled with revolutionary zeal, he was spoiling for a fight.

On 28 August *Révolutionnaire* fought no fewer than five British 74-gun ships-of-the-line. While completely dismasted, darkness allowed it to escape capture. (AC)

He got one. By 6:00pm *Révolutionaire* had fallen far enough back for *Bellerophon* to open fire on the French ship. Somehow, *Bellerophon*, normally the slowest ship in her division, had outpaced the other three 74s in the flying squadron. *Révolutionaire* had been launched in 1766 as *Bretagne*. Then a 100-gun ship, in 1794 it carried 110 guns. During the American Revolution it had been the flagship of the Brest Fleet. The struggle between *Bellerophon* and *Révolutionaire* was grossly uneven. Yet *Bellerophon* doggedly clung to the massive three-decker, fighting single-handed.

Howe saw the opening of the fight and 15 minutes after the gunnery duel began he signalled *Russell*, *Marlborough* and *Thunderer* to assist *Bellerophon*. It took the three an hour to reach the two ships. By then, French shot had damaged *Bellerophon*'s main cap, the junction of the main topmast and the topgallant mast set above the topmast. To keep the wounded mainmast from toppling, *Bellerophon* bore up, moving away from *Révolutionaire*, signalling an inability to continue fighting. *Révolutionaire* had taken damage too. Her mizzenmast had been shot away in the exchange.

By then *Russell*, *Marlborough* and *Thunderer* had come within range of *Révolutionaire* and started firing on her and the French ship immediately ahead of *Révolutionaire* from the windward side. *Révolutionaire* began to make sail and run before the wind to escape her tormenters. By then, *Leviathan* and *Audacious* caught up to *Révolutionaire*. They had been the lead ships on the windward of the two columns Howe had formed before signalling a general chase. These two ships had worked across the stern of the French line and were now upwind of the French, holding the weather gauge.

They swept down the previously unengaged windward side of the French column. Leviathan poured broadsides into *Révolutionaire* as it sailed past the three-decker, before attacking the French 74 ahead of *Révolutionaire*. *Audacious* stuck with *Révolutionaire*, firing into its lee quarter. The two ships remained closely engaged, with *Révolutionaire* losing its fore and main yards and main topsail yard. The only sail still set was its fore topsail. *Audacious* also suffered heavy damage to its rigging, which disabled it.

BELLEROPHON BRINGS *RÉVOLUTIONAIRE* TO COMBAT (PP. 58-59)

Révolutionaire **(1)** was spoiling for a fight. So was *Bellerophon* **(2)**. Both got what they wanted.

Bellerophon had the reputation as the fastest ship in the Channel Fleet. Commissioned in February 1793 by Captain William Pasley, he retained *Bellerophon* as his flagship when he was promoted to rear admiral and given command of the Flying Squadron, the four fastest ships-of-the-line in the Channel Fleet. *Bellerophon* had been sailing poorly over the months of 1794, however. Yet when the time came to engage a French three-decker, *Bellerophon* managed to outpace the other ships in the Flying Squadron, chiefly by clever sail handling.

Tacking towards the *Révolutionaire*, *Bellerophon* timed its turns to keep moving. As a result, it reached *Révolutionaire* well ahead of the rest of the fleet. The British 74 tackled the *Révolutionaire* single-handed, attacking the 110-gun ship on its lee quarter astern, and working its way forward, as shown in this plate.

It was a mastiff attacking a bear. While a powerful ship, *Bellerophon*'s guns threw a broadside of 829 pounds; *Révolutionaire*'s was 1,212 pounds. The two ships fought a single-handed duel for over 70 minutes before the other ships in the Flying Squadron finally caught up. Fortunately for *Bellerophon*, *Révolutionaire*'s gunnery was poor. Most of its shots flew high, cutting up rigging, without seriously damaging the masts. *Bellerophon* started a fire in *Révolutionaire*'s mizzen top and shot away the three-decker's mizzen by the time the other flying squadron ships reached gunnery range **(3)**.

By then damage to the supporting shrouds and a French hit in the cap of the lower main mast threatened to bring down *Bellerophon*'s main mast. *Bellerophon* broke off, falling away to windward. It repaired its damage, returning to battle the next day. *Révolutionaire* ended up being sent home due to damage it sustained from *Bellerophon* and the ships that took over the fight when *Bellerophon* broke off.

Bellerophon went on to be one of the most famous ships of the French Revolutionary and Napoleonic Wars. It fought at the Battle of the Nile (where it again fought a three-decker, *L'Orient*) and Trafalgar and was the ship which accepted Napoleon's surrender after the 100 Days. *Révolutionaire,* shattered on 28 May, would be scrapped two years later.

At 8:00pm, with sunset close at hand, Howe recalled his ships, signalling them to form line ahead and astern of the flagship as convenient. Soon that patch of ocean was temporarily clear of all ships but *Révolutionaire* and *Audacious*. At 10:00pm, the disabled *Révolutionaire* crossed the hawse of *Audacious*, threatening a collision. *Audacious* turned away avoiding the wounded but still dangerous *Révolutionaire*. As darkness fell, the guns fell silent. *Révolutionaire* had been badly damaged, losing nearly 400 men of a crew of 1,200. *Audacious'* crew claimed they saw *Révolutionaire* strike its colours, but the British ship was too badly damaged to take possession of the French three-decker. *Thunderer*, too, reported *Révolutionaire* was flying no colours when *Thunderer* crossed *Révolutionaire*'s stern. *Audacious* signalled *Thunderer* to take possession of the three-decker. *Thunderer*'s captain, more intent on obeying signals to re-form the battle line, let the opportunity pass, allowing *Révolutionaire* to escape.

HMS *Thunderer* was one of the 74s attacking *Révolutionnaire* on 28 May. This shows *Thunderer* late in its career. (AC)

Haze and rain screened theq battlefield as darkness fell. *Révolutionaire* lost its final mast sometime during the night. Villaret-Joyeuse discovering *Révolutionaire* missing sent the ship-of-the-line *Audacieux*, two frigates, and the brig-corvette *Unité* in search of his truant. Thanks to the weather, they would not find the three-decker until daybreak.

The day ended a draw, slightly favouring the British. *Révolutionaire* and *Audacious* were out of the battle due to damage, but *Révolutionaire* was a three-deck 110, while *Audacious* was a 74. Additionally *Audacieux* and *Unité* had to escort *Révolutionaire* back to Rochefort, *Audacieux* being detailed to tow *Révolutionaire*. The Channel Fleet was in good order while the Grand Fleet was in disarray. The two fleets spent the night steering parallel to each other. The British ships all carried a light in their stern, allowing their ships to remain in formation. None of the French ships bothered lighting themselves, increasing disarray.

BATTLE OF 29 MAY

The morning of 29 May dawned with the two fleets in sight, but not in combat. The two lines were six miles apart, with the French south of the British, still holding the weather gauge. The wind continued south by west, at the same force, or perhaps a little stronger than the day before. The better-practised British had gained on the French during the night. The 28th had dawned with the British van behind the French rear; by dawn on the 29th the British line overlapped the French line, with the lead ships in the British line reaching the French centre.

The Battle of 29 May

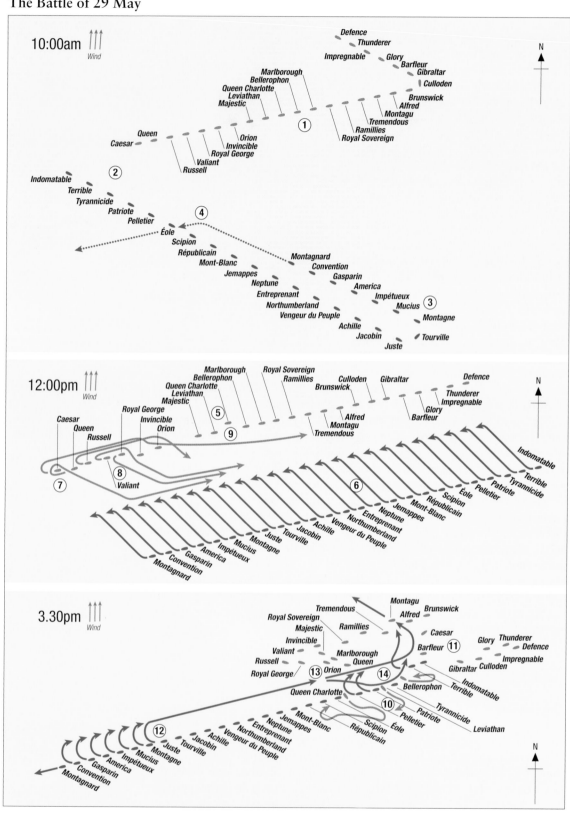

Révolutionnaire had been launched in 1766 as *Bretagne*. It served as flagship of the Brest Fleet at the Battle of Ushant in 1779. (Rama)

Several of the previous day's combatants were still on the previous day's battlefield, having been unable to clear it due to rigging damage. These were *Révolutionaire* and *Audacious*. *Révolutionaire* was a dismasted hulk and required assistance from the French fleet. It was found after sunrise and towed to safety as described earlier.

Audacious' masts were still standing, but its rigging was so badly damaged it could only run before the wind until repairs were made, and even then only slowly. Any strain on the masts would have brought them down. It slowly cleared the battlefield, headed towards the rest of the British fleet. Given its damage, the butcher's bill from the previous day's fight was surprisingly light: six killed and 16 wounded. During the night darkness and rain shrouded the ship, but at daybreak several French warships sent in search of *Révolutionaire* spotted *Audacious* crawling away. They set off in pursuit.

Audacious set all sail it could without bringing down its masts, running straight ahead without turning. Turning a sailing ship puts extra strain on the masts. Fortunately *Audacious* was running downwind, to the north in the direction of the British line. While the ship and brig-corvette broke off (presumably *Audacieux*, and *Unité* going to aid *Révolutionaire*), a frigate, the 36-gun *Bellone*, continued its pursuit. Firing into *Audacious'* stern, it clung to the battleship, perhaps hoping to dismast *Audacious* allowing it to capture an immobilized ship-of-the-line. *Bellone* finally broke away at 11:30am.

Audacious held its course for another 70 miles, before repairing its rigging enough to safely turn the ship. By then it was so far from the Channel Fleet as to make rejoining it impractical. It returned to England, reaching Plymouth on 3 June.

1. Howe orders the fleet to wear in succession to cross the French stern and gain the weather gauge.
2. British van and French rear exchange fire.
3. Villaret-Joyeuse orders the fleet to wear in succession, doubling back to protect his rear ships.
4. The French line turns parallel to the British line.
5. Howe orders the fleet to tack in succession intending to break the enemy line.
6. The French line closes on the British.
7. *Caesar* and *Queen* wear instead of tacking.
8. The rest of the van becomes disorganized, wearing or tacking individually.
9. Howe orders *Queen Charlotte* to break the enemy line, leading by example.
10. *Queen Charlotte*, *Leviathan* and *Bellerophon* break the enemy line near the rear.
11. The British rear engages the after two ships of the French line.
12. Villaret-Joyeuse takes *Montagne* out of line doubling back to protect the threatened rear ships, ordering the other French ships to form line-of-battle on the commander.
13. The French line closes on *Queen*. The British van moves to protect *Queen*.
14. The dismasted *Tyrannicide* is towed out of danger.
15. The French run downwind, yielding the weather gauge.

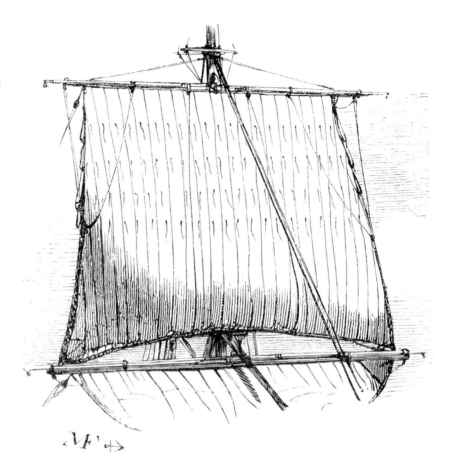

When dawn broke, *Caesar* led the British line, followed by *Queen*, *Russell*, *Valiant*, *Royal George*, *Invincible*, *Orion*, *Majestic*, *Leviathan*, *Queen Charlotte* and *Bellerophon*. Howe's signal of the previous night to form line as convenient had scrambled the order normally used. Howe's goal that day was to gain the weather gauge and the only practical way to do that was to pass through the French battle line.

At 7:30am, with the fleet on a larboard tack, and the wind coming from the port side, Howe signalled to pass through the enemy's line. The Channel Fleet tacked into the wind, changing its course 150 degrees and aiming to pass through the enemy's line, cutting off the French rear from the rest of the fleet. Five minutes later, Howe gave permission to fire on the enemy. The French rear opened fire on the approaching British, but at too great a distance to pose a threat. By 7:50am the British fleet was close enough to the French line that the lead British ships *Caesar* and *Queen* opened fire.

Villaret-Joyeuse saw the threat to his rear and at 8:00am he ordered the fleet to wear in succession. The French line doubled back on itself, with each ship turning where the lead ship had made its turn. It took an hour for the entire French fleet to make the turn. They were now heading west.

By 9:00am the French fleet had completed the turn, and was closing at a shallow angle with the British line of battle. The French still held the weather gauge. The French van again wore, bringing the two fleets into parallel lines. By 10:00am the vanguards of the two fleets were close enough to fire at each other.

Caesar, *Queen*, *Russell*, *Valiant* and *Royal George* opened fire and exchanged broadsides with the French. *Valiant* had luffed out of line, turning closer to the wind so it could close more quickly on the French. *Caesar*, on the other hand, kept its distance from the French line, even as next-behind *Queen* closed it.

At 11:30am Howe signalled to tack in succession to break the enemy's line. *Caesar*, the lead ship, was not carrying enough sail. A sailing ship's speed was dictated by the area of sail it had set. Up to a point, the greater the sail area the greater the speed. But as the wind grew stronger increasing sail area slowed a ship, and reducing the amount of sail increased its speed. A sailing ship heeled (rolled) in the direction opposite the direction of the wind. Once a ship heeled past a certain angle, it actually slowed. To keep it at that ideal angle ships would reduce sail area, either by taking in sails or by shortening sails. The sail area might also be reduced to prevent a strong wind from snapping a mast.

Shortening sail is exactly that – reducing the vertical height of a sail, making it shorter. Bands of reef points, short lines on the front and back side of the sail ran the width of the sail. By bringing the edges of the sails up to the spar at one of these reef bands sailors could tie the reef point around the spar, literally shortening the sail. Topsails on ships-of-the-line typically had three or four sets of reef bands on, and the courses (or lower sails) two.

Caesar had triple-reefed its topsails and fore sail, shortening about as much as possible without taking them in entirely. (A triple-reefed sail would use the bottom reef band on the topsails.) Additionally its mainsail had split and was being removed. *Caesar* was moving too slowly. Howe had signalled *Caesar*'s captain to make more sail, and move faster, but *Caesar* had responded with an inability signal.

Only the last few ships of the French rear would be caught if the British fleet tacked prematurely, so Howe cancelled the signal. The British line continued ahead on the course it held after the first turn. At 12:30pm, satisfied with the progress the British line had made, Howe repeated the signal to tack in succession.

By then smoke filled the battlefield and Howe's order to tack went unseen by the ships at the front of the line of battle. When, at 1:15pm, Howe signalled to engage the enemy and pass through their line, *Caesar*, the

Reefing a sail involved pulling the reef band to the spar and using the reef points to tie the sail to the spar. It was an all-hands exercise. (AC)

lead ship, signalled it was unable to tack and wore. This took *Caesar* away from the enemy as it started a 300 degree turn to reach the assigned heading. When it finally reached the British line of battle it was the eighth ship in line, rather than the first. *Queen*, having taken heavy damage to masts and spars through French fire in the hours spent closing on the French also signalled it was unable to tack and wore as well. The ships immediately behind *Caesar* and *Queen* failed to see the signal and continued on course.

Impatient, Howe decided to lead by example. With 'engage the enemy' signalled, he had *Queen Charlotte* tack towards the enemy. *Leviathan* and *Bellerophon* immediately ahead and behind Howe caught the spirit of Howe's example and joined him in a race for the French line.

Queen Charlotte broke the French line behind *Éole*, the sixth French ship from the rear of the French line, firing into her lee beam as *Queen Charlotte* slipped around *Éole*'s stern. *Bellerophon* passed the French line ahead of and *Leviathan* behind the 110-gun *Terrible* (a sister to *Révolutionnaire*, the ship *Bellerophon* attacked the previous day). *Terrible* had already lost its fore topmast in the gunnery duel earlier in the day.

Behind *Terrible* were *Tyrannicide* and *Indomptable*, which also had taken damage to their masts. They had suffered badly in the exchange of fire early in the battle when the British fleet closed on the French rear before the French reversed course. Both were lagging astern and drifting to leeward, bringing them close to the British line. Nearly crippled at that point, the two ships were attacked by the British vessels aft of *Queen Charlotte* in the line of battle, *Orion* and *Barfleur*. The French rear was in serious trouble, with at least three ships in danger of being taken.

Villaret-Joyeuse saw the danger. He ordered his van to wear, and come to the assistance of his rear. The column's lead ship, *Montagnarde*, ignored

Frustrated with the inactivity of the British van on 29 May, Howe took *Queen Charlotte* out of the British line of battle and broke the French line near the rear. Only *Leviathan* (left, hidden by smoke) and *Bellerophon* (right) supported Howe. (AC)

Lord Howe engaging the French Fleet under Adm. Villaret, on the 29.th May.

the order. It sailed resolutely ahead. Seeing the van's delay Villaret-Joyeuse ordered *Montagne* to break the line, wearing to come to the aid of the cripples in the stern. (Saint André did not object. As was his custom, he had gone below to wait in the hold when the battle started. He knew he was too important to risk getting injured.) The van ships, starting with the ship originally second and now in the lead, began to wear in succession.

This brought the French ships close to the crippled *Queen*. It had been the ship closest to the French van and had taken so much damage to its masts that it was barely under control. It could only continue straight ahead without risking bringing its masts down. As it was running parallel to the faster-moving French battle line, it was now at risk of capture.

The British van rushed to *Queen*'s assistance. The battle was devolving into a disorganized brawl. The van ships of both nations played tug-of-war around *Queen*. *Montagne* rushed to the aid of the French rear. *Queen Charlotte*, *Bellerophon* and *Leviathan*, having taken damage to their own rigging found that they were at risk of capture, with the British rear struggling to come to their aid.

Once the French cripples were rescued, Villaret-Joyeuse again ordered the French ships to wear around, this time heading west, and form a new line of battle downwind of the British. Howe, having mauled several ships in the French fleet, and gained the weather gauge, re-formed his line of battle, turning so the wind was on his port beam. Both fleets were running to the west. It was 5:00pm, and Villaret-Joyeuse and Howe both decided to end the fighting for the day. Howe had what he wanted most – an upwind position allowing him to attack the next day. Villaret-Joyeuse realized he was pulling the British fleet away from the precious grain convoy. Both were content.

Meanwhile also that day, 250 nautical miles west of Brest, the 28-gun British frigate *Caryfort* found a French-flagged frigate towing a Dutch

Howe's action forced Villaret-Joyeuse to take *Montagne* out of line to support the French rear. In the ensuing action, the fight devolved into disorder and the British gained the weather gauge. (AC)

merchant brig. *Caryfort* closed, the French frigate cast off its prize, and the two ships fought. After a 74-minute duel, the French ship struck. It proved to be *Castor*, captured by Nielly 20 days earlier. Commissioned as a French warship, *Castor* had departed from Nielly's squadron five days earlier, still carrying its British artillery and 20 members of the British crew.

The capture triggered a legal dispute over whether *Caryfort* had recaptured a British warship or taken an enemy warship. As a recaptured ship, *Castor* was 'salvage' with reduced prize money paid. The last battle of the campaign was a courtroom fight, with High Court of the Admiralty ultimately ruling that *Castor* was a legitimate prize over a year after the guns fell silent.

THE GLORIOUS FIRST OF JUNE, 30 MAY TO 1 JUNE

Both fleets had been battered by the action fought on 29 May. Fourteen Royal Navy ships-of-the-line had been engaged that day and four had taken significant casualties. *Caesar* had 22 men killed or wounded. *Queen* lost her captain, sailing master and 21 sailors killed or mortally wounded, with a lieutenant and 25 others wounded. *Royal George* had a lieutenant, midshipman and 15 sailors and marines killed and 21 wounded (including a midshipman). *Royal Sovereign* had eight killed and 22 wounded. *Queen Charlotte* had just one casualty; her sixth lieutenant was killed. With casualties in the other ships the butcher's bill for the Channel Fleet was 67 killed and 128 wounded.

Eleven ships had taken material damage: *Caesar, Queen, Russell, Royal George, Invincible, Orion, Majestic, Ramillies, Queen Charlotte, Defence* and *Royal Sovereign*. Most of the damage was to the masts and rigging. *Caesar*

Queen, *Russell* and *Invincible* had taken hits to the hull which created leaks. *Ramillies* had one gun dismounted. *Queen* had lost its mizzen topmast, and *Invincible* its main topmast. Both ships had taken other damage to their masts and spars, as had the other ships listed.

Although in many cases the damage was serious – masts shot through – it could be repaired at sea by the crew, given enough time. A mast shot through could be temporarily repaired by using spare spars to bridge the damage and bind the timbers together, much as one might splint a broken arm. A mast which had been shot off and lost overboard could be replaced by using a large spar as a substitute. Shot away cordage could be replaced or spliced. It required a skilled crew, but the Royal Navy had skilled crews. For example *Bellerophon* had fallen out of the battle on 28 May due to damage to its rigging. It had replaced or repaired the damage in time to take a major role in the fighting on 29 May. By 10:30am on 30 May, every British warship except *Caesar* reported they were ready for action.

The French suffered far more heavily. *Indomptable* was so badly battered only a dockyard refit could fix it. It was not fit to remain in a line of battle. *Tyrannicide* had lost all its topmasts, and could only set its lower sails. It was placed under tow, and remained under tow through the next three days. The French lacked both the skill and resources to replace the topmasts and topgallant masts. *Terrible* and *Éole* had suffered hull damage. Other ships had taken rigging damage during the long-range gunnery duel. It could be repaired but it would take time.

Villaret-Joyeuse took another hit after sunset. *Montagnard*, the lead ship that refused to turn during the battle of 29 May, disappeared. Villaret-Joyeuse

François Joseph Bouvet was the son of a captain of a French East India Company ship. A *lieutenant* for over eight years when the Revolution started, he was promoted to *contre-amiral* in 1793. He was Viilaret-Joyeuse's second in command in this campaign. (AC)

sent the frigate *Venus* after the fugitive, but it too failed to return. Two ships matching the description of *Montagnard* and *Venus* were spotted heading south-east during the night by British lookouts. The failure of both to return left Villaret-Joyeuse with 24 ships-of-the-line, two of them crippled, against what he believed were 26 British ships-of-the- line. (He believed *Charon*, a disarmed 44-gun two-decker serving as a hospital ship was a ship-of-the-line.)

He felt badly outnumbered, especially given the poor performance of his own crews the previous day. He got some succour after dark when *Trente-et-un Mai*, a 74, joined the fleet. Captained by Honoré Ganteaume, a future admiral, it had sailed independently from Brest on Ganteaume's initiative.

Fortunately for Villaret-Joyeuse there was no battle on the next day. As night fell the weather was foggy and stormy. The weather cleared after daybreak, remaining clear long enough for the two fleets to spot the other. Both sides prepared to fight another battle, but the weather closed in and shrouded both fleets in fog and rain. Howe was unwilling to initiate a fleet action in those conditions.

E. Howe breaking the French Line of Battle on the 1st of June 1794.

Villaret-Joyeuse was content to let the situation continue without coming to blows. He was moving north and west, with the British in pursuit. Every mile they followed him brought them a mile further from the grain convoy, which had passed close enough to Howe's ships to have been spotted if the weather had been clear on 30 May. Better still, on the night of the 30th, Villaret-Joyeuse got further reinforcements. Nielly, with the portions of his squadron not previously sent to Villaret-Joyeuse, arrived. This included three ships-of-the-line: *Sans Pareil*, *Trajan* and *Téméraire*. Nielly had rightly judged his ships would be more valuable reinforcing Villaret-Joyeuse than the convoy's escort.

Their arrival brought the total number of ships in the French line to 28. Having received four replacements, Villaret-Joyeuse decided he no longer needed the crippled *Indomptable*. He sent it back to Brest, accompanied by *Mont Blanc*. That brought his line of battle to 26 ships again. The next morning, at 9:00am when the fog lifted, the British were surprised to see all the ships in the French line of battle had undamaged rigging except one.

The British formed a line of battle, and approached the French. At 2:00pm Howe prepared to attack. The French edged away. Howe attempted to force an engagement, but the French kept off. At 7:00pm Howe realized if he did force a battle, it would continue on well after dark. Aware of the confusion of the previous two battles Howe wanted a fight during daylight, when his signals could be seen and he could keep better control. He hauled up, content to follow the French and start the battle the next day. He stationed a pair of frigates to keep an eye on the French in case they tried to slip away during the night.

That night both fleets rearranged their lines of battle. In the British line *Caesar* was still the lead ship, despite her shyness in the previous battle. Her captain was a friend of Howe's flag captain, who persuaded Howe to keep *Caesar* in the lead. Behind her were three of the ships of the flying squadron, *Bellerophon*, with Rear Admiral Pasley aboard, followed by *Leviathan* and *Russell*. Behind these was the fast-sailing *Royal Sovereign*, flying the flag of Thomas Graves, Howe's second-in-command. *Queen Charlotte* was the 14th ship in line with *Gibraltar* ahead and *Brunswick* behind her. Hood and his flagship, *Royal George*, was the 21st ship in a line of 25.

In the French line *Trajan* replaced the departed *Montagnard* as the lead ship, followed by *Éole*, *America* and *Témeraire*. Contre-Amiral François-Joseph Bouvet's flagship *Terrible* was next, having been moved to the van from the rear. Command of the French rear had been transferred to Nielly, who had shifted his flag from the *Sans Pareil* to the 110-gun *Républicain*. *Sans Pareil* and *Scipion*, from Nielly's old squadron made up the rear, replacing *Tryrannicide* (now in the middle two ahead of *Montagne* and being towed by *Trente-et-un Mai*) and the departed *Indomptable*. *Montagne* was the 13th ship in line with *Juste* ahead and *Jacobin* behind.

The first day of June dawned clear, with the wind moderate, perhaps 16 knots, from the south-south-east. The chop of the previous days was gone. The sea was smooth with long rollers. *Queen Charlotte* was at 47 degrees 48 minutes north, and 18 degrees 30 minutes west, or about 550 miles from Ushant. It would be the only major sailing era battle fought so far from land. The French fleet was on a larboard tack six nautical miles distant.

Howe wanted a battle. At 5:00am the British turned towards the French, steering north-west, and then at 6:15am due north. At 7:10am the fleet turned back to the west, on the larboard tack. Howe signalled to send the hands to breakfast. While they were eating Howe made two more signals – at 7:16am he signalled to engage the enemy, with a red pendant above the signal to indicate closer. At 7:25am he signalled to pass through the enemy line and attack to leeward. What Howe wanted was for his ships to fall on the French, and create a mêlée battle. At 8:12am, the meals finished, the

Villaret-Joyeuse's flagship, *Montagne*, was in the thick of the battle on 1 June. Despite the damage done to it after the two fleets collided, and despite its loss of a mast, the ship was able to escape capture. (AC)

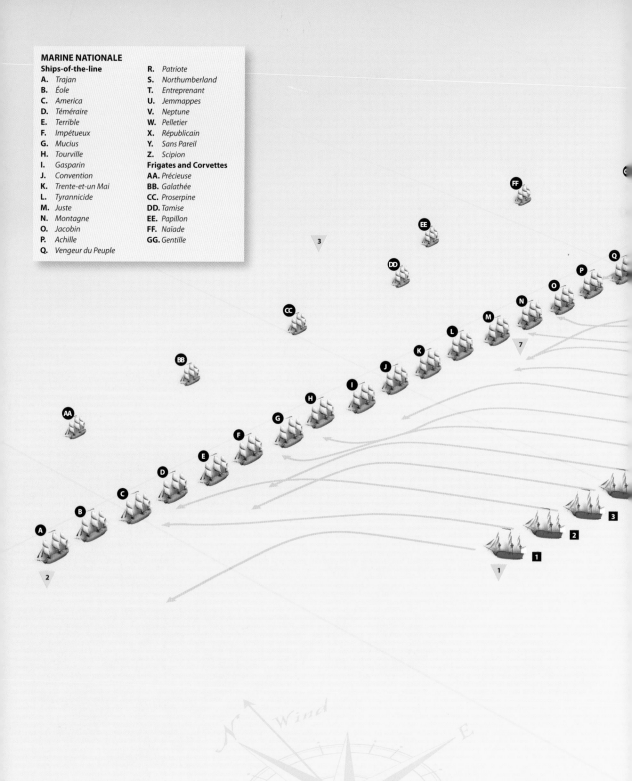

MARINE NATIONALE

Ships-of-the-line

A. Trajan
B. Éole
C. America
D. Téméraire
E. Terrible
F. Impétueux
G. Mucius
H. Tourville
I. Gasparin
J. Convention
K. Trente-et-un Mai
L. Tyrannicide
M. Juste
N. Montagne
O. Jacobin
P. Achille
Q. Vengeur du Peuple

R. Patriote
S. Northumberland
T. Entreprenant
U. Jemmappes
V. Neptune
W. Pelletier
X. Républicain
Y. Sans Pareil
Z. Scipion

Frigates and Corvettes

AA. Précieuse
BB. Galathée
CC. Proserpine
DD. Tamise
EE. Papillon
FF. Naïade
GG. Gentille

THE APPROACH TO BATTLE

The British and French fleets from lines of battle during the night of 31 May to 1 June and the British, who hold the weather gauge, move towards the French.

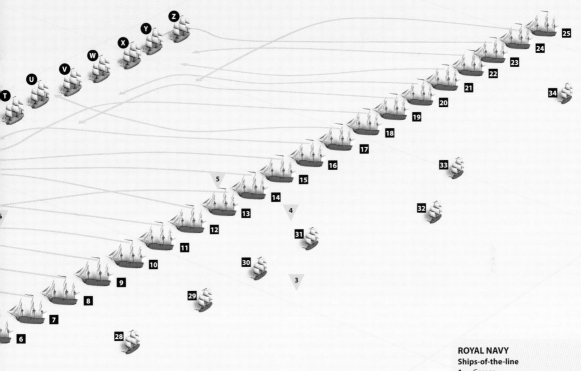

EVENTS

1. The British line of battle was led by *Caesar* followed by the three of the ships of the flying squadron, *Bellerophon*, *Leviathan* and *Russell*. Behind these was the *Royal Sovereign*, flying the flag of Thomas Graves, Howe's second-in-command. *Queen Charlotte* was the 14th ship in line with *Gibraltar* ahead and *Brunswick* behind. Hood and his flagship, *Royal George*, was the 21st ship in a line of 25.

2. In the French line, *Trajan* was the lead ship, followed by *Éole*, *America* and *Témeraire*. Contre-Amiral François- Joseph Bouvet's flagship *Terrible* was next. Command of the French rear had been transferred to Nielly in the *Républicain*. *Sans Pareil* and *Scipion* made up the rear.

3. Both fleets had two lines of frigates parallel to them to act as repeaters for the admirals' orders

4. At dawn on 1 June Howe began his preparations for battle. At 7:10am he sent the hands to breakfast and at 7:16am he signalled his ships to engage the enemy closer.

5. With breakfast finished the British fleet moved against the French and at 8:38am Howe signalled for his ships to steer for and engage the ship opposite them.

6. By 9:24am the British ships came within range of the French guns. By 9:50am French fire became general.

7. At 9:30am, *Queen Charlotte*, steering at an angle for *Montagne*, was fired on by *Vengeur*. *Queen Charlotte* responded to being fired upon to set its topgallants and fore sail to increase its speed to be the first to break the French line.

ROYAL NAVY
Ships-of-the-line
1. *Caesar*
2. *Bellerophon*
3. *Leviathan*
4. *Russell*
5. *Royal Sovereign*
6. *Marlborough*
7. *Defence*
8. *Impregnable*
9. *Tremendous*
10. *Barfleur*
11. *Invincible*
12. *Culloden*
13. *Gibraltar*
14. *Queen Charlotte*
15. *Brunswick*
16. *Valiant*
17. *Orion*
18. *Queen*
19. *Ramillies*
20. *Alfred*
21. *Montagu*
22. *Royal George*
23. *Majestic*
24. *Glory*
25. *Thunderer*

Frigates, fireships, and hospital ship
26. *Latona*
27. *Phaeton*
28. *Aquilon*
29. *Venus*
30. *Southampton*
31. *Pegasus*
32. *Charon*
33. *Comet*
34. *Niger*

For gun crews engaged in close combat on both sides, manning the guns on the gun deck was a noisy, smoke-filled and chaotic experience. (AC)

fleet turned and bore down on the French. At 8:38am Howe signalled for his ships to steer for and engage the ship opposite them. After that signal Howe closed his signal book and told the officers around him, 'And now gentlemen, no more book. No more signals.' All that was necessary was to resolutely close on the French.

Except some British ships seemed incapable of the necessary resolution. *Culloden* had backed its fore and main topsails, braking the ship. Howe was forced to signal *Culloden*, *Brunswick* and *Gibraltar* to make more sail. *Russell* and *Caesar* had also backed mainsails.

At 9:24am the British ships, especially *Defence*, which was moving faster than the other ships, came within range of the French guns. By 9:50am French fire became general. At 9:30am, *Queen Charlotte*, steering at an angle for *Montagne* was fired on by *Vengeur*. *Vengeur*'s fire was soon masked by *Brunswick*, which had obeyed Howe's signal and was surging forward. *Queen Charlotte* responded to being fired upon to set its topgallants and fore sail to increase its speed to be the first to break the French line.

Queen Charlotte crossed *Montagne*'s stern at 10:10am, firing a full broadside the length of the French flagship, killing 100 and wounding 200 men in its crew with this volley. *Jacobin* immediately behind *Montagne* had squeezed forward to cross *Queen Charlotte*'s bow, managing to shoot away *Queen Charlotte*'s fore topmast. The British flagship slipped between the two French ships, firing on *Montagne* with its port battery and *Jacobin* with the starboard.

Queen Charlotte was not the only British warship attacking. *Bellerophon*, *Leviathan*, *Marlborough*, *Defence*, *Invincible*, *Brunswick*, *Ramillies*, *Montagu*, *Royal George* and *Glory* all crossed the enemy line or attempted to. *Leviathan* ended up yardarm to yardarm with *America* on the upwind side, and *Brunswick* fouled *Vengeur* attempting to cross its bow. *Leviathan* battered its opponent to silence. While some ships, *Russell*, *Royal Sovereign* and *Culloden*, failed to get close enough to their enemy, only *Caesar* failed to close, content with bombarding *Trajan* from a distance.

Bellerophon was soon heavily engaged with *Éole* and then *Trajan*, which was allowed freedom to act by *Caesar*. *Bellerophon*'s gunfire proved equal to both its opponents which fled to windward, but not before shooting away

Bellerophon's fore and main topmasts. Rear Admiral Pasley was also hit and taken below with a leg requiring amputation. *Bellerophon* was forced to signal the frigate *Latona* for assistance. *Latona* towed *Bellerophon* off.

After silencing *America*, *Leviathan* set off to aid Howe, who was battling three ships (*Montagne*, *Jacobin* and *Juste*). *Russell* took possession of *America*, which had lost over a third of its crew.

Marlborough crossed astern of *Impétueux*, and then ranged up on the lee side. *Mucius*, behind *Impétueux*, came up on *Marlborough*'s disengaged side. A blistering action followed, where all three ships ended up dismasted, but which saw *Marlborough* silence both French ships. *Mucius* got a tow from another French ship and escaped, but *Impétueux* was eventually taken. *Marlborough* was eventually taken in tow by the frigate *Aquilon*.

Defence crossed the French line between *Mucius* and *Tourville* taking on both ships. *Mucius* eventually shifted its attention to *Marlborough*, and *Tourville* made off. *Defence* was soon engaged by three other ships-of-the-line from the French rear, including the three-decker *Républicain*. These ran to leeward at the approach of other British ships. *Defence* eventually received assistance from *Phaeton*.

Invincible crossed the line behind *Juste*, engaging her. *Juste* bore up to get away from *Invincible* stumbling into *Queen Charlotte*, After several broadsides from the flagship, *Juste* struck her colours.

Brunswick ended up locked in an epic battle with *Vengeur*. The two ships were so close together neither could run out their guns, instead firing with the muzzles against the bulwark of their enemy. The British blew off the gunports they could not open. The British, with flexible rammers, could load and fire faster than the French, who lacked space to ram home their shot. Both ships were rolling; the British timed their shots

Brunswick and *Vengeur de Peuple* ended up locked together and fought an epic gunnery duel for nearly an hour. Their bows were so close together that neither ship could open their bow gun ports. *Brunswick* blew its gun ports off, firing through its own gun ports. (AC)

Published by Bunney & co. 30 April 1800.

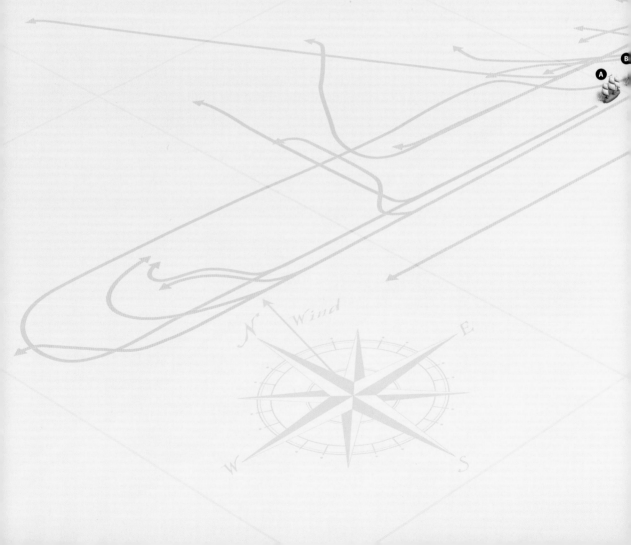

MARINE NATIONALE
Ships-of-the-line

A. *Trajan*
B. *Éole*
C. *America*
D. *Téméraire*
E. *Terrible*
F. *Impétueux*
G. *Mucius*
H. *Tourville*
I. *Gasparin*
J. *Convention*
K. *Trente-et-un Mai*
L. *Tyrannicide*
M. *Juste*
N. *Montagne*
O. *Jacobin*
P. *Achille*
Q. *Vengeur du Peuple*
R. *Patriote*
S. *Northumberland*
T. *Entreprenant*
U. *Jemmappes*
V. *Neptune*
W. *Pelletier*
X. *Républicain*
Y. *Sans Pareil*
Z. *Scipion*

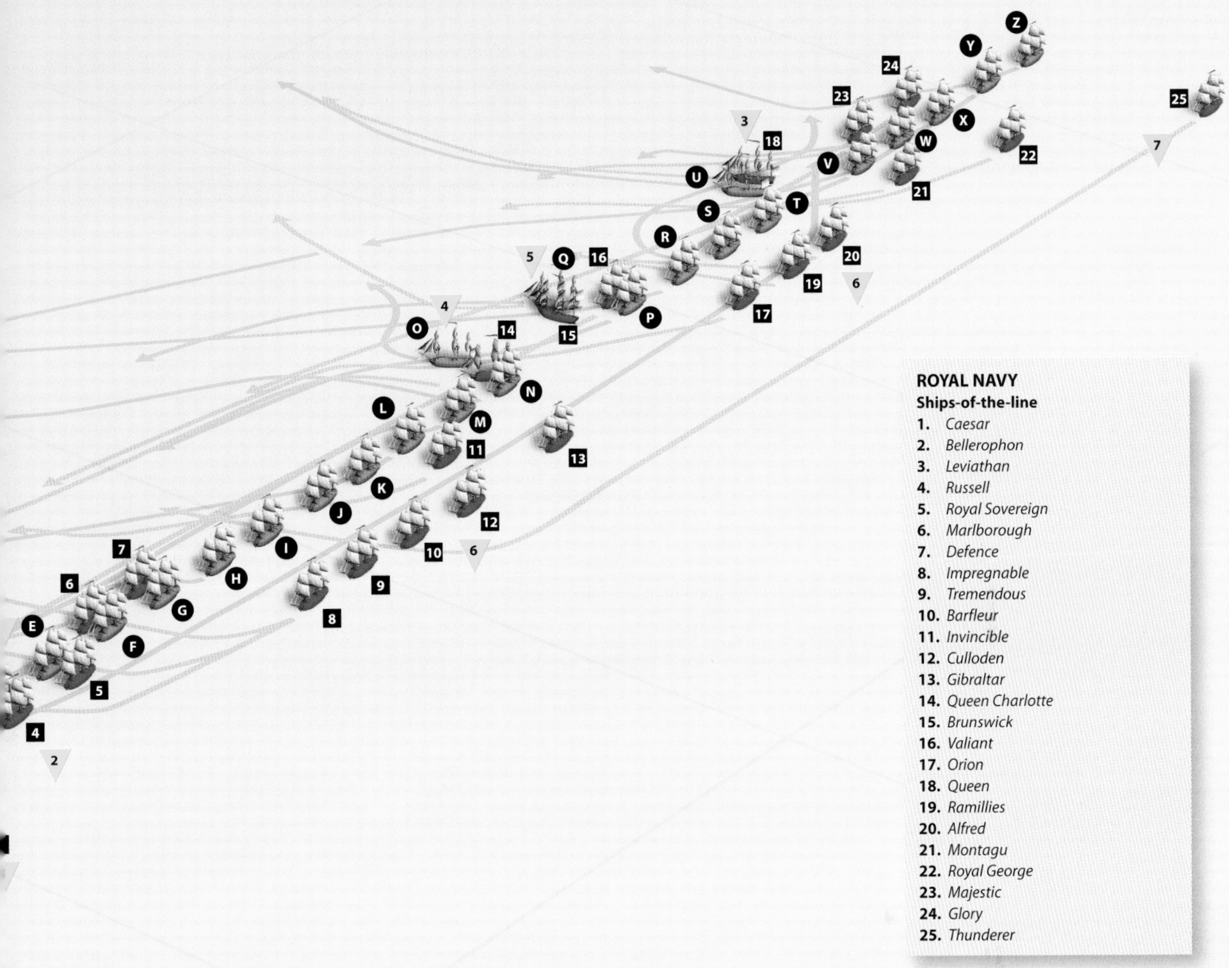

ROYAL NAVY
Ships-of-the-line

1. *Caesar*
2. *Bellerophon*
3. *Leviathan*
4. *Russell*
5. *Royal Sovereign*
6. *Marlborough*
7. *Defence*
8. *Impregnable*
9. *Tremendous*
10. *Barfleur*
11. *Invincible*
12. *Culloden*
13. *Gibraltar*
14. *Queen Charlotte*
15. *Brunswick*
16. *Valiant*
17. *Orion*
18. *Queen*
19. *Ramillies*
20. *Alfred*
21. *Montagu*
22. *Royal George*
23. *Majestic*
24. *Glory*
25. *Thunderer*

THE BREAKING OF THE LINE

With the British breaking the French line, the fighting becomes a close-quarters mêlée battle.

EVENTS

1. *Caesar* remains at long range and kept out of the fight, bombarding Trajan from a distance.

2. The next four ships in British van, *Bellerophon*, *Leviathan*, *Russell* and *Royal Sovereign* engage the French van on upwind side.

3. Six British ships break line and engage French broadside-to-broadside on lee side.

4. *Queen Charlotte* rakes *Montagne* and ends up fighting three French ships of the line.

5. *Vengeur* and *Brunswick* end up locked together, with the British ship's superior gunnery skills proving devastating in the close-range combat.

6. Eight British ships-of-the-line engage at a distance upwind of French fleet.

7. The British slow-sailers (*Royal George* and *Thunderer*) break French line later in the battle.

so one broadside fired on the downroll, plunging shot through *Vengeur*'s hull, and the next on the uproll, killing crew and disabling guns. *Vengeur* was reduced to a sinking condition, but its crew fought virtually until its decks were awash.

Valiant crossed the line ahead of *Patriote*, first ranging up along *Patriote* to windward. Half of *Patriote*'s crew was ill and the ship was silenced by *Valiant*'s broadsides. *Valiant* continued up the lee side of the French line engaging *Achilles* and dismasting her.

Queen had taken significant rigging damage approaching the French line, and was unable to catch her opposite, the French 74 *Northumberland*. Instead, she passed behind *Jemappes* and engaged it hotly for the next 30 minutes. Both ships lost masts, and *Queen*'s fire so battered *Jemappes* its crew surrendered. *Queen* was too disabled to take possession and the two ships drifted apart.

Royal George also passed through the French line, between *Sans Pareil* and *Républicain*, firing broadsides down the length of both ships as it passed. It then settled down to a gunnery duel with both ships. It was soon aided by *Glory*, a slow-sailing ship. *Glory* passed the French line behind *Scipion*, completely dismasting the French ship as it passed up the lee side. It then engaged *Sans Pareil*, knocking it out of the battle. Then it joined *Royal George* fighting *Républicain*. Both three-deckers raked the unfortunate *Républicain*, one ahead and one astern.

The rest of the British line failed to cross the French line, bearing up parallel to their French opposites to windward. In some cases this was because they interpreted the signals as advisory not mandatory. In others the ship's captain lacked the fortitude for close combat, or wished the option to maintain the weather gauge. This allowed those ships to escape by fleeing downwind.

Within an hour of *Queen Charlotte*'s crossing the French line the battle was effectively over. Twelve French ships were disabled, dismasted and hulled, surrounded by British warships. Another half dozen, including the flagship, *Montagne*, had taken serious damage aloft, combined with heavy crew casualties. These along with the rest of the French survivors had formed a new line of battle downwind of the original line. They were not in danger of being taken, but in no condition to rescue all of the disabled French warships, or even challenge the British further that day. All they could do was stand on the defensive.

The British could have pressed the battle further. They did not for three reasons. All of the ships with aggressive captains, the ones which broke the French line, were as immobile as the French. They needed to repair their rigging and masts. The ships which were capable of running down the French – well over a dozen – were commanded by men whose prudence outweighed their ferocity. Earlier in the day they let their desire to keep their ships safe override instructions to break the enemy's line. They could not be expected to behave boldly on their own initiative.

Finally Howe was exhausted. He was 68, and had spent the last four days on *Queen Charlotte*'s quarterdeck. The only rest he had enjoyed was in a chair placed on the quarterdeck for him. He had prizes to secure and his own crippled ships to assist. He did not want to lose control of the battle and was content to ride the victory he had just won.

Villaret-Joyeuse spent the rest of the day trying to rescue his cripples. He succeeded in sending frigates to tow off *Républicain*, *Mucius*, *Scipion* and *Jemappes*. Although seriously damaged, *Terrible* fought its way to freedom. *Vengeur*, its bottom literally blown out by *Berwick*'s gunfire, sank shortly after striking, before the British could reach the ship. Of its crew only 250 were plucked from the Atlantic. That left the British with six prizes: *Sans Pareil*, *Juste*, *America*, *Impétueux*, *Northumberland* and *Achille*. All were completely dismasted.

The butcher's bill was heavy. There were at least 2,500 French sailors killed and 4,000 taken prisoner. At least 5,000 French were wounded (including 690 of the prisoners). The British lost 290 killed and 858 wounded. Two British captains were killed and two admirals and one captain lost a limb.

For Villaret-Joyeuse it was an acceptable outcome. He had protected the convoy and kept his head attached to his shoulders. He doubted the British fleet, engaged in repairing its cripples and securing its prizes, would go after the convoy. He remained on the scene until evening, to allow further

MARINE NATIONALE
Ships-of-the-line

A. *Trajan*
B. *Éole*
C. *America*
D. *Téméraire*
E. *Terrible*
F. *Impétueux*
G. *Mucius*
H. *Tourville*
I. *Gasparin*
J. *Convention*
K. *Trente-et-un Mai*
L. *Tyrannicide*
M. *Juste*
N. *Montagne*
O. *Jacobin*
P. *Achille*
Q. *Vengeur du Peuple*
R. *Patriote*
S. *Northumberland*
T. *Entreprenant*
U. *Jemmappes*
V. *Neptune*
W. *Pelletier*
X. *Républicain*
Y. *Sans Pareil*
Z. *Scipion*

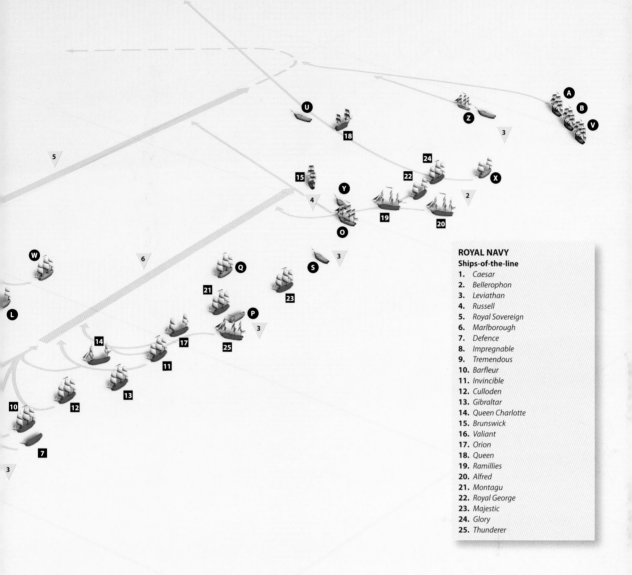

ROYAL NAVY

Ships-of-the-line
1. *Caesar*
2. *Bellerophon*
3. *Leviathan*
4. *Russell*
5. *Royal Sovereign*
6. *Marlborough*
7. *Defence*
8. *Impregnable*
9. *Tremendous*
10. *Barfleur*
11. *Invincible*
12. *Culloden*
13. *Gibraltar*
14. *Queen Charlotte*
15. *Brunswick*
16. *Valiant*
17. *Orion*
18. *Queen*
19. *Ramillies*
20. *Alfred*
21. *Montagu*
22. *Royal George*
23. *Majestic*
24. *Glory*
25. *Thunderer*

THE CLOSE OF THE BATTLE

In just over an hour the bulk of the fighting is done and the French
try to rescue their damage ships while the British collect their prizes.

▼ EVENTS

1. Mobile French warships escape to windward.

2. British ships capable of pursuit pursue.

3. Six French warships, Sans Pareil, Juste, America, Impétueux, Northumberland and Achille, strike to the British and are taken as prizes. All are completely dismasted.

4. Vengeur, having fought until its decks were awash, sinks.

5. Villaret-Joyeuse forms a new line of battle with his surviving uncrippled warships and waits there until sunset to allow uncaptured but crippled ships a rallying point.

6. Howe orders the British ships to form a new line of battle where the remaining ships can protect the prizes and crippled British warships, especially Queen.

7. The French depart to the north-west as night falls.

LORD HOWE ON THE QUARTERDECK OF THE *QUEEN CHARLOTTE* (PP. 82–83)

Why did Howe wish to break the French line and not just range up alongside? One advantage was that breaking the enemy's line permitted an opportunity for a raking broadside, one in which your shots ran the entire length of the enemy's ship. Such a broadside could devastate a ship, especially with a stern rake that passed through the glassed-in and panelled stern. The round bow planking meant some shots might hit at an angle, glancing off.

With a stern shot, unless the ball hit a deck beam, it would always penetrate the length of the ship. This could cripple a ship, especially when fired from a short range. Then, with the enemy's ship crippled, by coming alongside on the downwind side its escape could be checked.

Howe managed this on the First of June, sailing between the French flagship *Montagne* and its next astern *Jacobin*. While *Jacobin* managed to turn away from the wind to prevent being raked, Howe was able to unload a stern rake into *Montagne*, one

that left a quarter of *Montagne*'s crew casualties. Howe managed to lay along *Montagne*'s windward side, but aided by *Jacobin*, *Montagne* was able to slip out of Howes's trap and escape.

This plate shows that moment, even as Howe concentrated on managing the battle. With *Montagne* **(1)** in the background, Howe **(2)** can be seen in conference with his flag captain Roger Curtis **(3)** and *Queen Charlotte*'s master James Bowen **(4)**, as Howes's flag lieutenant, Edward Codrington **(5)** waits in the background. (All three would later become admirals.)

Behind Howe is an armchair **(6)**, brought up from Howe's quarters. Howe refused to quit the quarterdeck after initial contact on 28 May, determined to direct the battle. The chair was brought up for him to rest in that evening. By the time *Queen Charlotte* crossed *Montagne*'s stern, the 68-year-old Howe had been on the quarterdeck for four days. He would not go below until sunset on 1 June.

damaged ships to join him. Once he was sure the only French ships not with him were British prizes, he set course for Brest. A dismal day for France and a glorious day for Britain came to its end.

THE FLEETS SAIL HOME AND THE CONVOY ARRIVES

As the sun rose on 2 June 1794, the British held six prizes, and Howe had all the ships he began the battle with. Howe's concern was to keep things that way. At least a dozen of his ships needed repairs before they could sail again. Additionally, he had 4,000 French prisoners who needed to be prevented from recapturing their ships from whatever prize crews were placed aboard the prize ships.

The days of 2 and 3 June were spent making repairs on ships, both British ships and French prizes. Shot holes were plugged and hull damage patched, but the bulk of the attention was focused on replacing lost masts and spars. The ships were not going anywhere unless they could get sail on or were ignominiously towed to harbour. Additionally over the next two days the French crews were redistributed, scattered among the British warships in packets of 50 to 200 men.

Howe got some unexpected reinforcements. Thomas Troubridge and the bulk of his crew from *Castor* were being held prisoner on *Sans Pareil*, one of the captured ships. Once liberated, the frigate's men, along with Captain Troubridge, remained aboard to serve as the prize crew aboard the ship in which they had been captives.

The British sailors worked quite literally around the clock to repair their ships. It was not until 5:00am on 3 June that Howe felt ready to make sail. Even at that point a few ships were still so disabled as to require tows. *Queen* was one. While a task normally assigned a frigate, Howe gave the job to

Rain and storms shielded the Brest Fleet and the grain convoy from British view at critical moments. (AC)

Caesar, a sign of his disfavour due to its performance on 29 May and 1 June. Howe steered north-east, to the English Channel and home.

The trip took eight days. Finally on 11 June the Cornish coast was sighted. Howe detached nine ships, under the command of a badly wounded Thomas Graves, to Plymouth, where they arrived on 12 June. They carried the first word the public would hear of the battle. Howe arrived in Portsmouth at 11:00am on 13 June with the remaining 16 ships of his battle line and six French prizes.

Howe had completely ignored the French fleet, now down to 19 ships-of-the-line. The British lost contact with the French at 6:15pm on 1 June. Villaret-Joyeuse shaped a course to the north to escape the British. He left one frigate to watch the British. Gambling Howe would take his prizes and head for Britain, Villaret-Joyeuse set course for Brest. He felt he had executed his orders, and ensured the safety of the grain convoy. He must have crossed the path the British were to take ahead of them, and then was safely south of the now much larger Channel Fleet. With five of his surviving ships under tow he reached the approaches to Brest on 9 June. The two fleets must have been close to each other between 4 and 8 June, but never came within sight.

What Villaret-Joyeuse did spot as it neared Brest was Montagu's squadron. Montagu had been cruising independently seeking the French convoy. His orders were to rejoin Howe if he did not find the convoy by 20 May. His patrol line was south of the convoy's route, but he was getting reports it was near. He continued his patrol for a few days more. He failed to find the convoy, but had recaptured several ships from the Lisbon convoy.

When he finally attempted to rendezvous with Howe, Montague learned that Villaret-Joyeuse was at sea with the bulk of the Brest Fleet. Montagu's information indicated that Villaret-Joyeuse had over 20 ships-of-the-line, more than enough to sweep up Montagu's six ships-of-the-line. Howe was not at the rendezvous off Ushant when Montagu reached it and he gathered that Howe had gone west into the Atlantic.

Rather than sail in search of Howe, Montagu decided to sail to Plymouth. It was the course of prudence. Had Montagu sailed west he would have been as likely to find Villaret-Joyeuse as Howe, if he found any fleet at all – it would have been a difficult task in open ocean. Montagu reached Plymouth on 30 May.

The Admiralty wanted the French convoy intercepted. It sent Montagu back to sea, with orders to take station off Ushant. His squadron was reinforced with three new ships-of-the-line, the 74s *Colossus* and *Minotaur*, and the 64-gun *Ruby*. *Audacious*, battered by its fight with *Révolutionaire* on 28 May, finally reached Plymouth on 3 June. Armed with this new intelligence, Montagu weighed anchor on 4 June.

He arrived off Ushant early on 8 June. At 3:30pm he spotted 12 unknown sail in the east-southeast and gave chase. They proved to be eight French ships-of-the-line and four smaller French warships, commanded by Contre-Amiral Pierre-François Cornic. Cornic was a political appointment. He had not been in the Marine Royale in 1791, and had only a few months' experience as an admiral. When confronted by Montagu, Cornic took his squadron into Bertheaume Bay, under the guns of the fort there. Having chased the French into the bay, at 8:00pm Montagu stood off, waiting out the night off the entrance to Brest.

At 7:00am on 9 June, Montagu spotted Villaret-Joyeuse and his fleet headed towards the harbour. Although *Républicain*, *Terrible*, *Scipion*, *Mucius* and *Jemappes* were dismasted, the French fleet still had 14 French ships-of-the-line capable of fighting. Villaret-Joyeuse gave chase with these.

Had Howe pursued Villaret-Joyeuse, the Brest Fleet would have been caught between Howe's hammer and Montagu's anvil. Instead, Montagu, aware of Cornic's force nearby, formed line of battle and fell away from Villaret-Joyeuse. While Cornic remained mewed up in Bertheaume Bay, Montagu was still badly outnumbered. Two of his ships, *Ganges* and especially *Alexander*, were slow sailers. By 5:00pm after having chased Montagu since 9:30am, Villaret-Joyeuse had closed to within four nautical miles of *Alexander*. Then worried he was drawn too far away from his crippled ships, Villaret-Joyeuse broke off the action. He anchored off Bertheaume Bay, alongside Cornic's squadron, later that evening.

Montagu lost sight of Villaret-Joyeuse at 6:00pm. He stood to the northwest, seeking Howe (who by then was east of Montagu). At 4:00am on 10 June, he turned to the Channel. On 12 June, he reached Plymouth, where he joined the nine ships sent there with Graves.

As for the grain convoy, it had been doggedly sailing north-east since leaving the Chesapeake. By 25 May it was running east between 47 and 48

Plymouth Dock from Mount Edgcumbe

When Admiral Graves' detachment reached Plymouth (shown) on 3 June with word of the battle, Montagu took his squadron, reinforced by three more ships-of-the-line, back to Brest in search of the grain convoy. (USNHHC)

The route of the French Grain Fleet

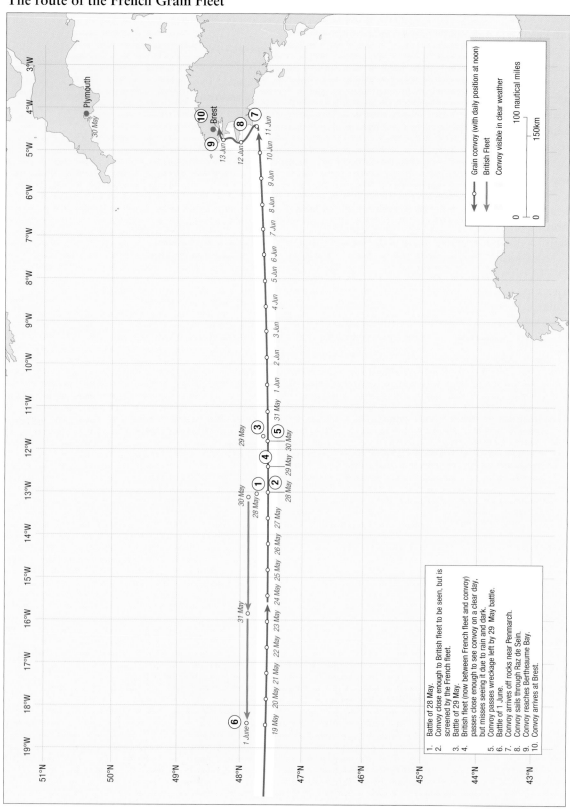

Legend:
- Grain convoy (with daily position at noon)
- British Fleet
- Convoy visible in clear weather

0 — 100 nautical miles
0 — 150km

1. Battle of 28 May.
2. Convoy close enough to British fleet to be seen, but is screened by the French fleet.
3. Battle of 29 May.
4. British fleet (now between French fleet and convoy) passes close enough to see convoy on a clear day, but misses seeing it due to rain and dark.
5. Convoy passes wreckage left by 29 May battle.
6. Battle of 1 June.
7. Convoy arrives off rocks near Penmarch.
8. Convoy sails through Raz de Sein.
9. Convoy reaches Bertheaume Bay.
10. Convoy arrives at Brest.

degrees and north, the precise latitude Howe had been taking the Channel Fleet. A collision had been avoided by Howe's turn north on 26 May. Had Howe run another 50 to 100 nautical miles west he would have collided with it. The convoy was slightly south of, and few nautical miles west of, the location where Howe and Villaret-Joyeuse battled on 28 May.

As it was, in the afternoon of 30 May, the convoy sailed through the wreckage left by the battle on the 29th. It was also joined by the wayward *Montagnard* that day and then by *Mont Blanc*, raising the size of the escort to four ships-of-the-line. It is likely that the Channel Fleet had sailed between the Brest Fleet and the grain convoy on 30 May, with both French formations shielded from British view by rain and fog. Howe's attention was fixed north, on the Grand Fleet. Villaret-Joyeuse's northward drift pulled Howe just far enough away from the convoy to allow the vulnerable merchantmen to avoid detection.

As alarming as sailing through the wreckage was, Van Stabel decided to press on. It was the correct decision. Had he doubled back he could well have sailed into the British on 31 May or 1 June. The convoy sailed through empty ocean for the next two weeks.

Van Stabel was concerned enough about the British that he did not sail directly for the harbour of Brest. Rather he set his landfall for the Penmarch, a cape 30 nautical miles south of Brest's entrance. Once there he scouted north to ensure Brest was not covered by a hostile fleet. On the night of the 12th the French in Bertheaume Bay spotted lights in the Raz de Sein, the passage between Île-de-Sein and Cap Sizun on the Breton mainland, the southern passage to Brest. The grain fleet had finally arrived, unmolested by the British.

The same day Montagu arrived at Plymouth, the ships of the grain convoy were working their way into the Outer Water. Over the next two days, covered by the Marine Nationale, the ships of the convoy passed through the Goulet into Brest Harbour. On 14 June, they were joined by the covering warships. The campaign was over.

Against the odds the grain convoy arrived at the entrance to Brest on 14 June, virtually intact. Only one ship had been lost, and that foundered due to the weather. (AC)

AFTERMATH

Howe and the Channel Fleet returned to a heroes' welcome. It was the first clear major victory for Britain since the war started. And major it was. Sinking or capturing seven ships-of-the-line meant the battle fought on 1 June had been the biggest British naval victory since Quiberon Bay in 1759. In terms of assets it could be considered bigger. At Quiberon Bay six French ships-of-the-line had been destroyed and only one captured. Additionally two British ships-of-the-line were wrecked at Quiberon Bay. Howe lost no ships.

George III took the unprecedented step of visiting the Channel Fleet in Portsmouth on 26 June, something he had never done before and would never do again. He visited Howe aboard *Queen Charlotte* in Spithead, and presented Howe with a diamond-hilted sword (valued at £3,000) and a gold chain to be worn around the neck. The king dined aboard the flagship with Howe that night. The next day George III held a levee where the fleet's officers were presented.

Royal favour fell on other flag officers, too. All the admirals received gold chains. Graves was made an Irish peer and Hood elevated to a British viscount (Lord Bridport). Bowyer, Gardiner, Pasley and Curtis (Howe's flag

King George III was so pleased by the victory he came to Portsmouth, visited Howe at his flagship and presented him with a diamond-hilted sword and a gold chain on *Queen Charlotte's* quarterdeck. It was the only time the king made such a visit. (AC)

captain, who had been promoted to rear admiral after the battle) were made baronets. Bowyer and Pasley, both of whom had lost a leg on 1 June, were awarded annual £1,000 pensions.

The first lieutenants of every ship-of-the-line present at the three days' worth of battles were promoted to commander, as were several flag lieutenants. Parliament voted its thanks. Additionally, everyone in the fleet received a share of the £201,096 prize money awarded.

France also hailed the battle as a magnificent victory. Saint André, wrote a glowing account of the victory for *Le Moniteur*. The grain convoy reached France untouched. *That* was the important thing. French officers from the fleet paraded in Paris with food brought from America. The seven ships-of-the-line lost were treated as victories, proof of the French sailors' fidelity to the revolution.

Vengeur became legend. Bertrand Barère, a member of the National Convention, gave a speech in the Assembly hailing the willingness of the crew to fight until the ship sank under them. He claimed that preferring death to capture, they had died to a man. Subsequently, Jean François Renaudin, captain of *Vengeur*, along with his son (an officer aboard *Vengeur*) and some of the other 250-odd survivors were returned to France in September 1794 in a prisoner exchange. Renaudin had been 'posthumously' promoted to *contre-amiral* the month before.

Virtually everyone associated with the battle – on both sides – did well. Sainte André and Villaret-Joyeuse enjoyed long careers. The captains, both British and French, proved a constellation of the naval stars of the next 20 years of warfare. Present were John Duckworth, James Gambier, Charles Cotton, and Cuthbert Collingwood among the British officers and Jean-Baptiste-François Bompart, Bertrand Keranguen, Honoré Joseph Antoine Ganteaume, and Louis l'Héritier for the French. All went on to greater glory and achievements.

Only Anthony Malloy, captain of *Caesar*, came off badly. His failure to engage closely led to whispers that he was a coward. He asked for a court martial to clear his name. In 1795 the court ruled he was not a coward, but he lacked professional judgement. He was dismissed from *Caesar*, and never employed again.

THE BATTLEFIELD TODAY

Today there is little to mark the first major fleet action of the French Revolutionary Wars. Not one of the ships that fought at the battles fought on 28 May, 29 May and 1 June – or even any of the subsidiary battles surrounding the campaign – still exists. All were broken up or had sunk long ago. Not one was preserved as a museum ship. Only artefacts remain.

A few lasted well into the 19th century. *Montagne*, renamed *Ocean*, remained in French Navy (as it bobbed between the names Marine Nationale, Marine Impérial and Marine Royale, depending on who was in power) until 1856, when it was finally broken up. *Tremendous*, a 74, survived past the centenary of the battle. It was renamed *Grampus* in 1845, and survived as a Royal Navy ship until it was sold out of service in 1897, 113 years after it was launched. *Sans Pareil*, taken as a prize that day, was purchased and served in the Royal Navy until it was broken up in 1842, the longest-lived of all the prizes.

The campaigns three main actions were fought further from land than any major fleet action during the entire age of fighting sail. The action of 28 May was fought 364 nautical miles west of the western tip of Ushant, that of 1 June, 550 nautical miles. It was simply too hard to find a fleet transiting the ocean in the era before radar, radio, and aircraft. Only fortune brought Howe to Villaret-Joyeuse, and that after two weeks of search.

Given the three battles' location in the mid-Atlantic there was no cape, strait or headland to give the battles their names. Inevitably they were named after the days on which they were fought: The Battle of 28 May, the Battle of 29 May and the Battle of 1 June. (For the British. The French, with their revolutionary calendar named them Bataille du 9 prairial an 2, Bataille du 10 prairial an 2, and Bataille du 13 prairial an 2, or simply Combat de Prairial for all three.) It was probably equally inevitable, that in Britain the final battle became the Glorious First of June.

The grey Atlantic waters over which these three battles were fought would not see that magnitude of combat again until World War II, during the Battle of the Atlantic. The cause would again be protecting and attacking convoys as surface raiders and U-boats sought out merchant convoys bound between Europe and America. They would be guarded by destroyers, frigates and corvettes deadlier than the ships-of-the-line of the French Revolution-era, while still being among the weakest oceangoing naval combatants of World War II.

Sea lanes cross the Atlantic near these locations. It remains a natural route for travelling from Baltimore to Brest, or really anywhere from a port on the Atlantic seaboard of the United States to somewhere in France, England or

any European port requiring passage of the English Channel. The ships are larger than they were in 1794, built of steel rather than wood, powered by diesel engines instead of wind, and travelling at least ten knots (if they still use nautical miles instead of metric measurements) instead of two knots.

If you are travelling across the Atlantic today aboard a ship, and you have a GPS receiver, it can tell you when you pass the places where these battles were fought. Yet grey water would be the only thing visible. No other trace remains.

Sans Pareil was only a year old when captured by the British. It spent the next 48 years as a Royal Navy warship. This painting of HMS *Sans Pareil* was made after the end of the Napoleonic Wars. (AC)

FURTHER READING

The most comprehensive account of war between the Marine Nationale and the Royal Navy is one of the earliest – the six-volume *The Naval History of Great Britain from the Declaration of War by France in 1793 to the Accession of King George IV* by William James. James gives balanced accounts of the battles, with less chest-thumping than normally encountered. I obtained a set of the 1859 volume (it was originally published in 1822–24) in the 1980s, which I relied upon heavily. (Volume 1 covers the period of this campaign.) Two other major sources were William Laird Clowes *The Royal Navy, A History from the Earliest Times to the Present*, Vol. 4 (Sampson, Lowes, Marston and Company, London 1897–1901) and Alfred Thayer Mahan's *The Influence of Sea Power upon the French Revolution and*

LORD HOWE they run, or the British Tars giving the Carmgnols a Dressing on Memorable 1st of June 1794

The reaction to the victory in Britain was jubilant. This period cartoon, showing British tars routing cowardly French sailors, was typical, and ignored the courage shown by the French crews. The caption 'Lord Howe they run...' makes a pun on the admiral's name. (LOC)

Empire: 1793–1812, Volume 1, (Boston, Little, Brown, and Company, 1894).

The social history of both the Royal Navy and the Marine Nationale, general information on shipbuilding practices, administration, and the strategic situation was extracted from Clowes, and the writings of N.A.M. Rodger, especially *Command of the Ocean: A Naval History of Britain 1649–1815* (W.W. Norton and Company, New York, London, 2004) and E. H. Jenkins's *A History of the French Navy From its Beginnings to the Present* (MacDonald and Jane's, London, 1973).

An excellent (and recent) source on manpower in the Royal Navy (and other navies of the period) is *The Myth of the Press Gang: Volunteers, Impressment, and the Naval Manpower Problem in the Late Eighteenth Century,* by J. Ross Dancy (The Boydell Press, Woodbridge UK, 2015).

Several 19th-century French sources were used: Eugéne Pacini's *La Marine, Arsenaux, Navires, Équipages, Navigation, Atterranges, Combats* (Paris, 1844), *Campagnes, Triomphes, Revers, Désastres et Guerres Civiles des Français de 1792 a la Paix de 1856* by F. Ladimir, F. and E. Moreau (Paris, 1856) and *Histoire Nationale de la Marine et des Marins François,* (Paris 1880) by Jules Trousset.

Other books used include:

Cordingly, David, *Billy Ruffian: The Bellerophon and the Downfall of the Napoleon, The Biography of a Ship, 1782–1836,* Bloomsbury Publishing, London, 2003

Cormack, William S, *Revolution and Political Conflict in the French Navy, 1789–1794,* Cambridge, New York: Cambridge University Press, 1995

Jacksonn, T. Sturges, editor, *Logs of the Great Sea Fights 1794–1805,* Vol. 1, Navy Records Society, 1894

Van Der Merwe, Pieter, *Science and British and French Navies 1700–1850,* National Maritime Museum 2005

Warner, Oliver, *The Glorious First of June,* New York, The Macmillan Company, 1961

Winfield, Rif, *British Warships in the Age of Sail, 1714–1792: Design, Construction, Careers and Fates,* Seaforth Publishing, Barnsley, South Yorkshire, 2008

Winfield, Rif, and Roberts Stephen S., *French Warships in the Age of Sail 1786–1861: Design, Construction, Careers and Fates,* Seaforth Publishing, Barnsley, South Yorkshire, 2015

Winfield, Rif, and Roberts Stephen S., *French Warships in the Age of Sail 1626–1786: Design, Construction, Careers and Fates,* Seaforth Publishing, Barnsley, South Yorkshire, 2017

Most of the 19th-century sources can be found online at http://archive.org/ or at Google Books (http://books.google.com/).

Numerous other sources were used, but space precludes listing them. One online site which may interest aficionados of the sailing era is Three Decks – Warships in the Age of Sail (http://www.threedecks.org/). While not a final authority, it has much of interest.

INDEX